A004590503

CW00821131

GREAT TREASURES OF THE WORLD

Produced by AA Publishing

© The Automobile Association 1997
Maps © The Automobile Association 1997

ISBN 0 7495 1207 5
A CIP catalogue record for this book is
available from the British Library

Published by AA Publishing (a trading name of Automobile Association Developments Limited, whose
registered office is Norfolk House, Priestley Road, Basingstoke, Hampshire RG24 9NY;
registered number 1878835)

Author: Nance Fyson
Copy editor: Wendy Dallas
Picture researcher: Kathy Lockley

Colour separation by Fotographics Ltd
Printed and bound in Spain by Graficromo, Cordoba

Acknowledgements

The Automobile Association wishes to thank the following libraries and photographers for their assistance in the preparation of this book:

AGENCE PHOTORAPHIQUE DE LAS RÉUNION DES MUSÉES NATIONAUX 94/5, 95, 105; PHOTO AKG LONDON 8, 64/5 (Erich Lessing), 65a; COURTESY OF A LA VIELLE RUSSIE 70/1, 71b; COURTESY DEPARTMENT OF LIBRARY SERVICES, AMERICAN MUSEUM OF NATURAL HISTORY 20a (K 9849), 80/1 (5003(3) John Bigelow Taylor); ASHMOLEAN MUSEUM, OXFORD 104, 116b; AA PHOTO LIBRARY F/cover The Mask of Tutankhamun (R Strange), 17b (C Coe); AY R. MAS (ARXIU MAS) BARCELONA 62/3, 63, 83, 90/1; BAYERISCHES NATIONAL MUSEUM 40; BILDARCHIV PREUSSISCHER KULTURBESITZ, BERLIN 34 (Antikenmuseum, Staatliche Museen, Ingrid Geske-Heiden), 35a (Antikensammlung, Staatliche Museen zu Berlin, Johannes Laurentius), 34/5 (Antikenmuseum SMPK Berlin, Ingrid Geske-Heiden); BOLTIN PICTURE LIBRARY 2b, 11, 24/5, 25b, 80a, 80b, 81; THE BRIDGEMAN ART LIBRARY 2c Gold Standing Cup (Kremlin Museums, Moscow), 14 Bronze dagger decorated with gold, from the Royal Tomb IV, Mycenae, Bronze Age (National Archaeological Museum, Athens), 14/5 Gold mask from the Acropolis of Mycenae, 16C BC (National Archaeological Museum, Athens), 44/5b, 45a, 45c, 45d Viking jewellery, silver necklace bearing a pendant in the form of Thor's hammer, gold brooch, twisted gold ring, gold brooch (Nationalmuseet, Copenhagen), 46/7 Shoulder clasp from the Sutton Hoo Ship Burial, Anglo-Saxon c625–30 AD (British Museum, London), 50a, 50b Maya plaque, c700 AD, pre-Columbian (Museum of Mankind, London), 56a Dancing Shiva, bronze, South Indian, 19–20C (Oriental Museum, Durham University), 57 Siva Nataraja bronze figure, Chola Dynasty, late 11C (Christie's, London), 65b Reliquary statue of Saint Foy c980 (Church of Ste Foy, Conques, France/ Lauros – Giraudon), 67 The Crown of St Steven of Hungary (Magyar Nemzeti Galeria, Budapest), 77b Dunstable Swan, enamelled gold version of Henry IV's Swan Badge (British Museum, London), 82b Beaten gold nose ornament from Calima, late 14C (British Museum, London), 96a Gospel cover, gold with repousse and enamel decoration, set with jewels, Russian 12C (Kremlin Museums, Moscow), 96b Gospel cover, embossed silver with filigree, enamel and engraved decoration, Moscow, 1499 (Kremlin Museums, Moscow), 96c Cover for the 1797 Acts of the Apostles and Book of the Gospels, silver with filigree decoration, late 18C (Kremlin Museums, Moscow), 97 Crown of Karen, engraved gold set with jewels, fur trimming, niello and openwork mid 16C (Kremlin Museums, Moscow), 98b French jewelled enamelled pendant formed as Hercules, Paris c1540 (Christie's, London), 102b German table clock, brass-gilt circular canister case with engraved hour figures and central sun (Worshipful Company of Clockmakers' Collection), 103b Drum clock, Nuremberg c1590 (British Museum, London), 108 Sconce, single light in Anglo-Dutch style of restoration period 1668–90 (Private Collection), 109a Wager cup by John Angell, 1827 in form of woman holding cup above her head (Private Collection), 113a Pomander, decorated with chased scrollwork enclosing black enamel, silver gilt c1580 (Asprey & Co, London), 113b Gold pomander, enamelled and set with precious stones, French c1600 (Sotheby's, New York), 114 Inro showing a servant kneeling before a Samurai: signed by Jitokusai Gyokuzan (Wrangham Collection), 115a, 115b Tobacco Pouch with Hiramaki-e design, signed Zeshin: Inro foxes wedding procession in Sumi-Togidashi; signed Toyo; Inro, two sages reading a scroll in Sumi-e Togidashi, signed Kanshosai, boating on a lake executed in Togidashi, signed Shiomi Masanan, Inro duck on a river bank in Takamaki-e, signed Jokasai (Wrangham Collection); 115c Inro with Pine, Bamboo and Plum decoration, laquered wood, coral and shell Japanese, late 18/19C (Oriental Museum, Durham University), 116a The Phoenix Coronet, Empress's hair piece from the Ding tomb, Beijing, Ming Dynasty (1368–1644) (Zhang Shui Cheng), 120a, 120b, 121a, 121c Collection of half hunter pocket watches, 19C (Christie's, London), 124a, 125 Louis XV Ormolu chinoiserie clock mounted with tole figures in the form of a Chinese child and a man with Vincennes porcelain flowers by Jaques-Jerome Gudin and later movement by James Grohe (Partride Fine Arts, London), 124b Lyre clock, white marble ormolu with paste jewels, French c1810 (Usher Gallery, Lincoln), 126a Louis XV oval gold agate and enamel snuff box, by Gabriel Gallois, Paris 1738 (Private Collection), 126b A Frederick Augustus III Hardstone porcelain and gold snuff box by Johann Christian Neuber, Dresden 1775 (Christie's, London), 127a Collection of gold boxes from the Rothschild Collection (Christie's, London), 130a Table screen, Chinese 18C (jade) (Private Collection), 130b Table screen, Chinese 18C, (Spink & Son Ltd), 135 Ashanti leather helmet, with attached gold and silver leaf decoration (Museum of Mankind, London), 136/7 Folding fan, depicting exotic pheasants amid flowers, Chinese, Macao, c1850 (Fitzwilliam Museum, University of Cambridge), 138 Silver soup tureen by Paul Storr (Victoria & Albert Museum, London), 139a Silver teapot showing bucolic figures in style of Teniers, by Edward Farrell, London (Victoria & Albert Museum, London), 139b Silver soup tureen by Paul Storr with Egyptian motifs, 1807 (Christie's, London), 140b The Aberdeen Jewel, jewelled and enamelled gold locket with lock of hair said to be that of Mary Queen of Scots, late 16C (Private Collection), 140c Renaissance pendant jewel (Christie's, London), 141 The Gresley Jewel with minature portraits of Sir Thomas Gresley and his bride Catherine Walsingham (Hilliard, Nicholas 1547–1619), (Victoria & Albert Museum, London), 142/3 Gold and enamelled turban ornament from Jaipur, India, early 19C (Victoria & Albert Museum, London), 147 Magnolia vase by Tiffany & Co, 1893, enamelled silver (Metropolitian Museum of Art, New York), 148a, 148b, 148c, 148d Collection of Faberge pocket watches (Christie's, London), 151a Art nouveau pendant in the form of a butterfly, enamel and soap-stone c1900 (Private Collection), 151b Hair comb by Fred Partridge (horn, enamelled copper & moonstones) (Cheltenham Art Gallery & Museums, Gloucestershire), 155a Cartier diamond bracelet with pave-set links (Bonhams London), 155b Art deco diamond teardrop clip brooch, French (Bonhams London); COPYRIGHT BRITISH MUSEUM, LONDON 12, 18, 22, 22/3, 25a, 31a, 36, 38a, 38b, 38/9, 48, 49, 74, 75, 136; CAMERA PRESS LTD 106b (C Beaton); CHRISTIE'S IMAGES 150a, 150b, 150c; THE CLEVELAND MUSEUM OF ART 142 (Locket designed to hold perfume cloisonné enamel on gold, H.5.7 cm. India, Jaipur c1700. Gift of the Twentieth Century Club, 60.198); CROWN COPYRIGHT IS REPRODUCED WITH THE PERMISSION OF THE CONTROLLER OF HMSO 106a, 107; THE EGYPTIAN MUSEUM 16a, 16c, 17a; E T ARCHIVE 1, 2a, 5a, 5c, 17c, 20b, 21, 26a, 26b, 30/1, 44b (Historisk Museet Norway); FITZWILLIAM MUSEUM CAMBRIDGE 5b; THE FORBES MAGAZINE COLLECTION, NEW YORK, all rights reserved, 3 (Larry Stein), 149b (Eric Landsberg); WERNER FORMAN ARCHIVE LTD 45b, (Upplandsmuseet, Uppsala), 51 (National Museum of Anthropolgy, Mexico City), 56b (Philip Goldman Collection), 85a (British Museum, London), 85b (British Museum, London); PHILIPPE GARNER 146; GERMANISCHES NATIONAL MUSEUM 93; GIRAUDON 58; GOLDSMITH'S HALL 152/3a, 153, 154a, 158; GÜNTER MEYER FOTO-WERBESTUDIO 154b; ROBERT HARDING PICTURE LIBRARY 10b (British Museum, London), 15, 16b, 16d, 27, 32/3, 33a, 33b, 54, 55, 78 (British Museum, London); HIRMER FOTOARCHIV 10a, 23; MICHAEL HOLFORD 28a, 28b, 29a, 29b, 36/7, 37a, 37c, 46, 47, 79, 84, 134, 149c, 158/9; KUNSTHISTORISCHES MUSEUM, VIENNA 42, 59, 77a, 86/7, 94, 100, 117; KUNSTINDUSTRIMUSEET, COPENHAGEN 126c, 152/3b (Ole Woldbye); KUNSTINDUSTRIMUSEET, OSLO 140a; LANDESMUSEUM, MAINZ 68/9; STANISLAW MICHTA 100/1; DAS MUSEUM IM AUGUSTINER-STOCK 122/3, 123a; COURTESY MUSEUM OF FINE ARTS, BOSTON 13 (Gift of Mrs W Scott Fitz), 128/9; MUSEUM FÜR VOLKERKUNDE 78/9; NATIONAL MUSEUM OF THE AMERICAN INDIAN 82a, 144/5, 145; NATIONAL-MUSEET DENMARK 30a; NATIONAL MUSEUM OF IRELAND 31b, 52; THE TRUSTEES OF THE NATIONAL MUSEUMS OF SCOTLAND 53b; ORTHODOX CHURCH MUSEUM OF FINLAND 71a; PHOTOTHÈQUE DES MUSÉES DE LA VILLE DE PARIS 19; ROCKROSE 156 (H Kaston); SCALA 41, 43, 60, 60/1, 72, 73, 76, 86, 98a, 110, 110/1; SCIENCE MUSEUM/SCIENCE & SOCIETY PICTURE LIBRARY 102a, 103a; SCIENCE PHOTO LIBRARY 9a (V Fleming), 9b (R de Gugliemo): SPINK & SON LTD 131; STATENS HISTORISKA MUSEUM 44a, 44/5a (Christer Ahlin); BY COURTESY OF THE BOARD OF TRUSTEES OF THE VICTORIA & ALBERT MUSEUM 53a, 66,68, 88a, 88b, 89, 90 (D P P Naish), 91 (D P P Naish), 92, 99, 109b, 112/3, 118, 123b, 127b, 132, 133, 149a, 157a (D P P Naish); THE WALLACE COLLECTION 119a, 119b, 134/5; THE TRUSTEES OF THE WEDGEWOOD MUSEUM, BARLASTON, STAFFORDSHIRE 121b

Cover illustrations: The mask of Tutankhamun; the Bayeux Tapestry

Contents

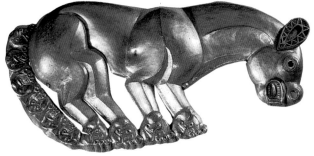

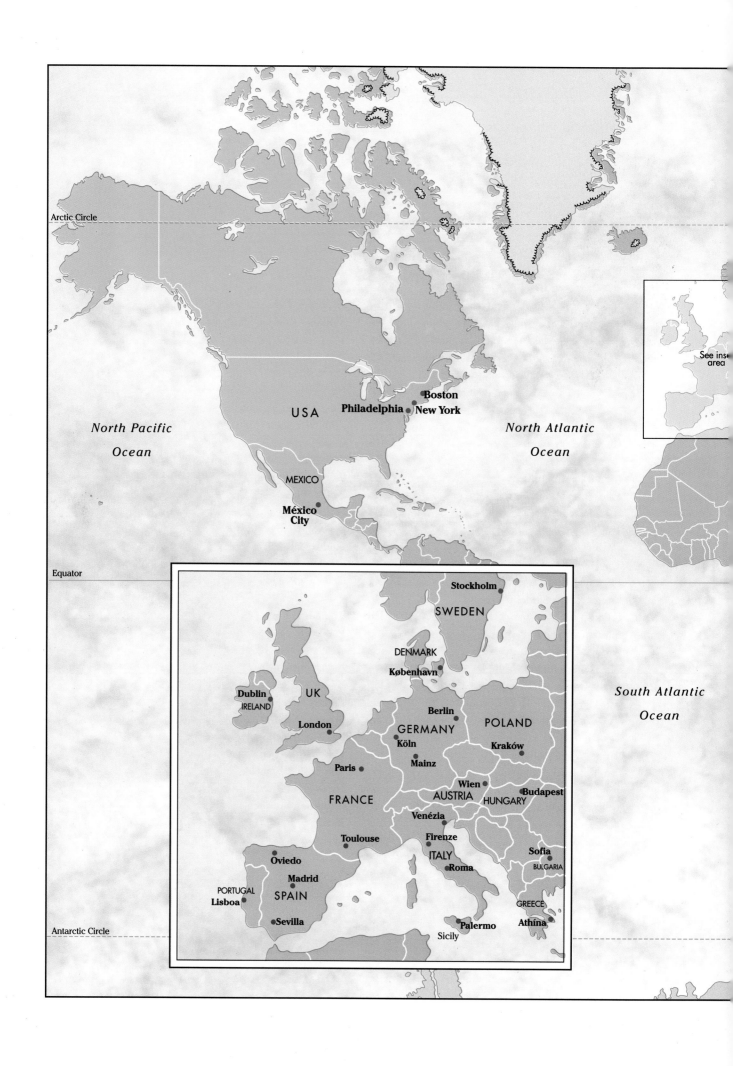

Arctic Circle

North Pacific
Ocean

USA

Boston
Philadelphia • New York

North Atlantic
Ocean

See ins
area

MEXICO

México
City

Equator

Stockholm
SWEDEN

DENMARK
København

South Atlantic
Ocean

Dublin
IRELAND
UK
London

Berlin
GERMANY   POLAND
Köln   Kraków
Mainz

Paris
Wien   Budapest
FRANCE   AUSTRIA   HUNGARY
Venézia
Toulouse   Firenze
Sofia
Oviedo   ITALY   BULGARIA
Madrid   Roma
PORTUGAL   SPAIN
Lisboa   GREECE
•Sevilla   Palermo   Athína
Sicily

Antarctic Circle

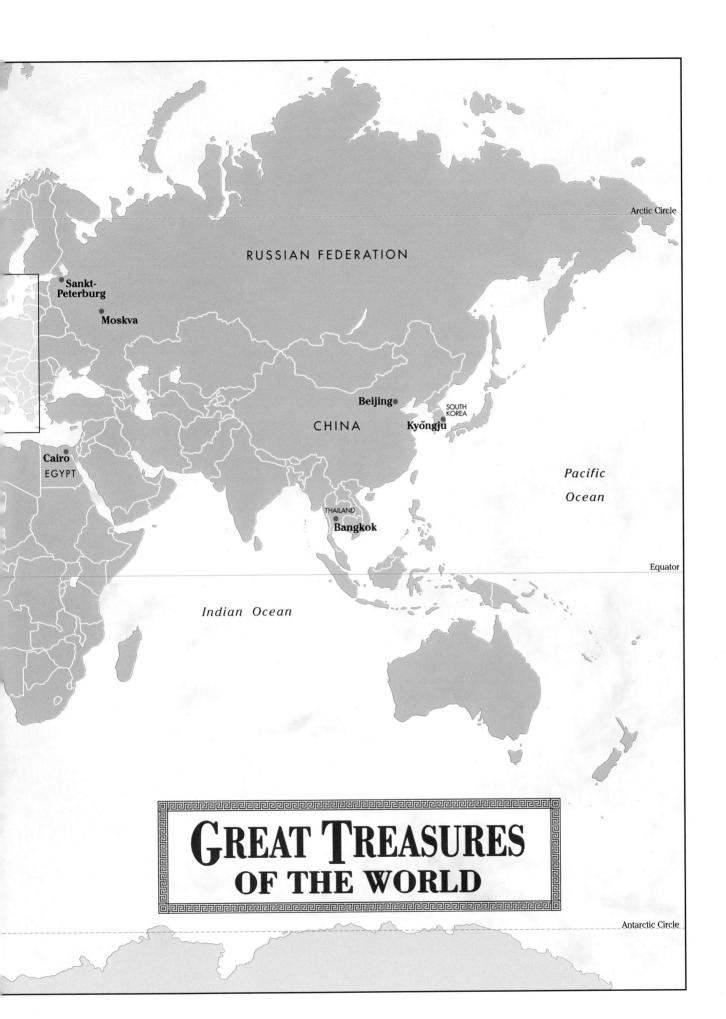

Arctic Circle

RUSSIAN FEDERATION

Sankt-
Peterburg

Moskva

Beijing

SOUTH
KOREA

CHINA

Kyŏngju

Pacific

Ocean

Cairo

EGYPT

THAILAND

Bangkok

Equator

Indian Ocean

GREAT TREASURES
OF THE WORLD

Antarctic Circle

Precious Metals and Gems

Glittering metals arrayed with colourful gems have fascinated and attracted people since ancient times. Gold has been sought in every part of the world for over 6,000 years, yet its scarcity value remains: all of the gold ever recovered would make a cube no more than about 20 yards (18m) square. About three-quarters of this quantity has been reclaimed from the earth in only the last 500 years.

Archaeological remains show that gold was being worked by skilful craftsmen as early as 3000 BC around the Middle and Near East. While gold is too soft for fashioning into tools, its malleability makes it ideal for working into decorative objects and jewellery. A single ounce of gold can be hammered into a single sheet over 100 ft (30m) square – or drawn into a length of wire 50 miles (80.5km) long. Gold is not subject to corrosion, oxidation or attack from common acids and it does not tarnish or rust. Gold nuggets shimmering in the sun are, however, little more than a romantic fantasy.

Ancient craftsmen first joined pieces of metal by riveting, pinning or literally sewing them together with gold wire, but the discovery of soldering techniques in Mesopotamia in the 3rd millennium BC provided a much faster and stronger means of fixing. The soldering process itself is one of the most basic of metalworking and lapidary techniques, but it has helped craftsmen to produce a magnificent range of artistic creations over the centuries.

Just as gold has provided the raw material for many of the world's great treasures, so precious and semi-precious stones have been used for thousands of years to create articles of great beauty and worth. Diamonds are among the most valued precious stones, and are also the hardest substance known. The main sources were originally India and Brazil, but South Africa and other African countries, Siberia and Venezuela have now taken the lead as the world's most important diamond producers. The colour of diamonds varies considerably: those used in jewellery range from white to a bluish tinge and from shades of yellow to brown.

While gold and diamonds are among the most expensive materials used to create great items of jewellery and ornamentation, a wide variety of other metals, stones and even organic substances (such as coral, pearls and ivory) have also been used. Most of the techniques used today have been practised since the time of the ancient civilisations of Mesopotamia, and the forms created (from necklaces, rings and earrings to bowls, decorated weapons and religious objects) have remained much the same. The skilled way in which all these substances have been modified and combined makes a fascinating catalogue of artistic achievement.

Above, sapphires panned from river gravels, smoothed and rounded by abrasion and, right, crystals of native (naturally-occurring) gold, found in veins of quartz

Bull's Head from Ur

A richly embellished harp ornamented with a fine bull's head, dating from about 2800 BC, was among treasures found in the royal cemetery at Ur in Mesopotamia. This was one of the major centres of Sumerian civilisation, south of what is now Baghdad in Iraq. Mesopotamia occupied the valleys between the Tigris and Euphrates rivers, and was divided into city-states such as Ur, each of which had its own ruler.

At its height from about 3500 to 2300 BC, Ur was a city of temples, palaces and public buildings. Excavations of the site began in the 1920s and were led by British archaeologist C L Woolley, who spent over five years exploring the area. Work by the University of Pennsylvania has yielded many more objects, among them the harp which is now housed in the university's museum. The extensive haul from royal tombs at Ur included gold and silver statues, vessels, weapons and inlaid jewellery – all revealing the fine craftsmanship of this ancient civilisation.

The bull's head makes lavish use of lapis lazuli, which was the favourite stone of the Sumerians. Their literature and mythology constantly praised its beauty, and the difficulty of obtaining pieces of workable size must have added to its worth. The death goddess of the Sumerian underworld held court in a palace of lapis lazuli, and the love goddess wore jewellery made of the stone.

Other fine treasures were found in the grave of Mesilim, King of Kish. From Mesilim's shoulder hung a gold dagger, its hilt carved from a single piece of lapis lazuli studded with gold, and his skull was found resting in a gold helmet beaten so thin that it was as flexible as paper.

Among the other remarkable gold artefacts found in the graves at Ur was a strange carving of a billy goat raised on its hind legs and resting against a tree. It stands about 20in (50cm) high, its face and legs made of thin sheet gold with lapis lazuli and shell used to create the impression of fleece and shoulders, eyes and horns. The carving is now housed in London's British Museum.

An enormous amount of jewellery must have been looted over the centuries from the tombs at Ur, as only one grave was found intact by Woolley and his team. Nonetheless, an impressive range of personal ornaments worn by both men and women has been recovered. The most splendid tomb belonged to Queen Pu-Abi, who was buried complete with her servants to attend her in the afterlife. Woolley discovered 63 bodies in the outer chamber of the tomb, all lying in neat rows and dressed in exquisite gold jewellery. The Queen herself was in an inner chamber, draped in gold and semiprecious stones, such as lapis lazuli, cornelians and agate.

REPOUSSÉ

One of the oldest techniques for incorporating design into metal is called repoussé, in which a pattern is raised in relief by hammering from the underside. Gold's malleability allows it to be beaten wafer thin and decorated in high relief without fracturing.

The gold is first laid on a bed of warm pitch and the design is drawn on the back using a scribe tool. A variety of blunt chisels are used to punch out the design. The pitch stops the whole object from caving in when pressure is applied to a small area. During the process the metal is toughened by heat treatments which prevent it from becoming brittle. The object can then be taken from the pitch and worked on from the front using chasing tools to add finer details.

LEFT:
Harps originated in ancient Egypt and, like other musical instruments, were often decorated by the Sumerians. This bull's head, made from a thin layer of gold leaf over wood and ornamented with lapis lazuli, was found on a harp in a royal tomb at Ur.

Minoan Snake Goddess

RIGHT:

The Master of Animals is barely 2½in (6cm) high and is hammered out in thin gold. Many examples of Minoan jewellery from the 17th century BC were found on the island of Aegina.

The Minoans were a sophisticated race who inhabited the Aegean island of Crete from about 3000 to 1100 BC. The British archaeologist Sir Arthur Evans explored their territory in the early 1900s and named the island civilisation after Minos, the legendary King of Crete. At its dazzling height, 2000 to 1450 BC, Minoan culture produced royal palaces such as Knossos and a range of fine artefacts.

No temples were built and religious worship seems to have taken place at outdoor altars. An ivory goddess holding gold snakes represented the central deity in their religion. She was often shown wearing a revealing gown, as in the small statuette opposite, now in the Museum of Fine Arts, Boston. Ivory carving using tusks from Syrian elephants (which became extinct in the 9th century BC) was one of the arts practised in Minoan palace workshops.

The Middle Minoan phase came to a sudden end in about 1650 BC when an earthquake struck the island. The rebuilding of its towns and cities marked the start of the Late Minoan phase. Minoan civilisation finally ended in about 1450 BC, when the invading Mycenaeans came from the Greek mainland and pillaged towns and palaces.

Besides small statues in ivory, the Minoans were known for their genius in delicate metalwork, exemplified by bronze, gold and silver horns and drinking cups decorated with relief bands. Shown here is a gold pectoral, an ornament worn on the breast, which was made sometime in the period 1700–1550 BC and is now in the British Museum.

It depicts a nature god standing in a field of lotuses and holding water birds in both hands. Called the 'Master of Animals', the pectoral was part of the celebrated Aegina Treasure. This collection was found in a Mycenaean tomb on the island of Aegina, but it consisted of Minoan objects of the 17th and 16th centuries BC. These included necklaces, pendants, hairpins and diadems – some using beads of cornelian, rock crystal, green jasper and amethyst – and magnificent gold finger rings inlaid with lapis lazuli.

Another famous Minoan jewel from around the same time is a gold pendant from a tomb at Mallia showing two bees at a honeycomb.

Gold seals were another favourite form of Minoan jewellery: as well as being used for stamping identification in wax, they were regarded as lucky or magical charms. One fine example, made between 1700 and 1550 BC, is intricately carved with a design of two goats mating. Fish and insects provided other popular themes.

PECTORALS

In ancient Egypt decorative 'pectorals' were often hung on the breast from a ribbon or chain, or placed on mummies as funerary ornaments. They were still being worn in the Middle Ages, when they were usually sewn on a garment, or fixed with a pin like a brooch. A cross worn on the breast was referred to as a pectoral cross, while pectoral discs, often hammered out in gold and decorated with figures, were suspended on a cord or string of beads.

A fine example is the Pectoral of the Universe, now in the Regional Museum, Oaxaca, Mexico. This Mixtec Indian object from about AD 1000 is from the Monte Alban Treasure and has seven vertically linked sections made from cast gold.

The Mask of Agamemnon

Several splendid gold death masks were uncovered by Heinrich Schliemann at Mycenae on Crete in 1876. What he called the Mask of Agamemnon, dating from about 1500 BC, was undoubtedly the finest treasure of the group. Its dignified expression, closed eyes and elegantly groomed beard and moustache suggest a ruler of some importance. Later examination has shown this mask to be about three centuries too early to be that of Agamemnon, but the original association with the famed Mycenaean king has remained.

Mycenaean power was waning by about 1200 BC, their cities conquered by about 1100 BC. An important collection of Mycenaean art is now housed at the Greek National Museum in Athens

BELOW:

Mycenaean tomb treasures included bronze daggers inlaid with gold images of animals and hunting scenes.

RIGHT:

Heinrich Schliemann was convinced that one tomb mask found at Mycenae was that of King Agamemnon; however, it was later discovered to be a tribute to a ruler as yet unidentified.

INSET:

A gold 'kantharos' bowl from Kalamata, dating from the 16th century BC.

The Mycenaeans, successors to the Minoans of Crete, were leading traders around the Aegean Sea and built large fortified towns. A complex social hierarchy included artisans and metalworkers who served mainly the wealthy upper class. Their conquests after 1500 BC included not only Crete but also Rhodes, Cyprus and the Cycladic Islands.

Mycenaeans buried their royalty in shaft graves, which they filled with gold and silver vessels and weapons, carved amber and ivory, jewellery and other objects. Some corpses were mummified, their faces covered with gold masks, as practised in ancient Egypt (see page 16). In the later years of Mycenaean rule, kings and nobles were buried in large tombs, and it was the greatest of these, containing the Treasure of Atreus, which was uncovered at Mycenae by Schliemann.

and includes the stylish Mask of Agamemnon and the bronze dagger, also shown here, which is inlaid with gold. Such daggers often had finely shaped gold hilts.

The personal story of the treasure seeker Heinrich Schliemann is itself a fascinating tale. As a boy in Germany he greatly admired the epic poems of Homer, which he believed to be accurate accounts of events that had taken place in ancient Greece. A successful career in business brought Schliemann consider-able wealth and allowed him to indulge his curiosity about ancient sites. In 1871 the now 50-year-old Schliemann concluded from the description in Homer's *Iliad* that a mound in

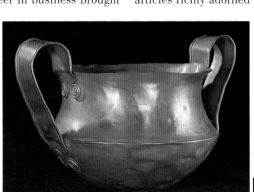

northern Turkey contained King Priam's ancient city of Troy. He did find gold artefacts and other items there, and, although it turned out that they were not in fact from Priam's Troy, the success of his find spurred him to seek other ancient sites. Homer mentioned Mycenae, the Golden City of King Agamemnon – Schliemann's next great quest. Digging in southern Greece, he found a series of shaft graves carved out of rock, which held gold articles richly adorned with precious stones. Gold burial masks and breastplates had been placed over the male bodies, while females had been ornamented with gold discs. The bodies of several small children were found wrapped in gold foil.

TROJAN TREASURE

In the early 1870s Heinrich Schliemann spent over three years excavating a site at Hissarlik in present-day Turkey thought to have been King Priam's Troy. Suddenly he spotted metal gleaming in the sun. He dismissed his labourers and dug with the help of his wife.

A staggering array of gold items – including rings, earrings, bracelets and vessels – was unearthed. The greatest prize was two diadems, one made from over 16,000 pieces of gold chain. Schliemann believed this to be the crown of Helen of Troy, but in fact the 8,000-piece treasure has since been dated to 2500–2200 BC, which was 1,000 years before King Priam. During World War II the items were lost and have never been recovered.

ABOVE:

A figure of the jackal-headed Egyptian god Anubis. Associated with death, he was the guardian of the necropolis.

BELOW:

The falcon pectoral found in the tomb was decorated with inlays of lapis lazuli, turquoise, cornelian and light blue glass, with obsidian eyes. The falcon was a symbolic representation of the sun god Ra.

TREASURES OF KINGS

Treasures found in the tombs of nobles and kings have greatly increased modern knowledge about ancient Egyptian life. It was in about 1567 BC that the princes of Thebes regained control of Egypt and founded the New Kingdom, which began with the 18th Dynasty. This included the reign of Tutankhamun and lasted until about 30 years after his death, when a new dynasty was founded by Rameses I (opposite, below). Many treasures from this Kingdom, including Tutankhamun burial objects, are now in Cairo's National Museum. Egyptians believed in life after death and the necessity of taking material possessions into the next world. Tombs were packed with remarkable treasures, and even walls were decorated with scenes depicting possessions and pleasures – all intended to accompany the dead into the afterlife.

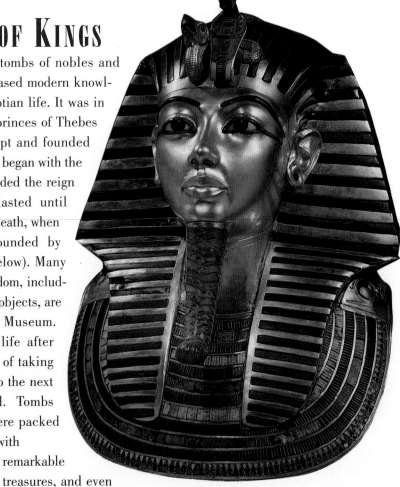

THE ROYAL TOMB

Tutankhamun's tomb is one of the best-known treasures of the world and the only nearly-intact tomb of ancient Egyptian royalty that has been uncovered. Located in the Valley of the Kings at Thebes, it was revealed in 1922 by an Englishman, Howard Carter, whose team found a burial tomb containing four chambers. An ante-chamber held such priceless objects as chariots, jewels and gold-inlaid furniture. The mummy of Tutankhamun and other precious objects lay within an inner chamber. The king's sarcophagus (far right) is a particularly good example of the way lapis lazuli (see panel) was used to mark

AMUN

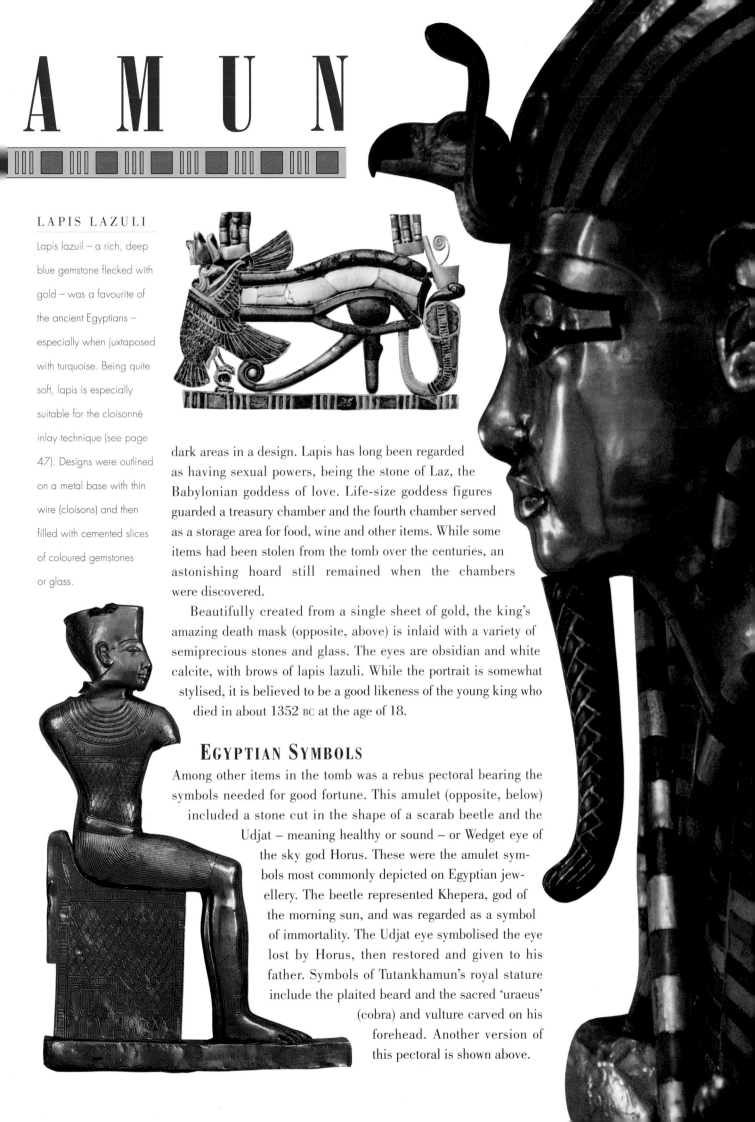

LAPIS LAZULI

Lapis lazuil – a rich, deep blue gemstone flecked with gold – was a favourite of the ancient Egyptians – especially when juxtaposed with turquoise. Being quite soft, lapis is especially suitable for the cloisonné inlay technique (see page 47). Designs were outlined on a metal base with thin wire (cloisons) and then filled with cemented slices of coloured gemstones or glass.

dark areas in a design. Lapis has long been regarded as having sexual powers, being the stone of Laz, the Babylonian goddess of love. Life-size goddess figures guarded a treasury chamber and the fourth chamber served as a storage area for food, wine and other items. While some items had been stolen from the tomb over the centuries, an astonishing hoard still remained when the chambers were discovered.

Beautifully created from a single sheet of gold, the king's amazing death mask (opposite, above) is inlaid with a variety of semiprecious stones and glass. The eyes are obsidian and white calcite, with brows of lapis lazuli. While the portrait is somewhat stylised, it is believed to be a good likeness of the young king who died in about 1352 BC at the age of 18.

EGYPTIAN SYMBOLS

Among other items in the tomb was a rebus pectoral bearing the symbols needed for good fortune. This amulet (opposite, below) included a stone cut in the shape of a scarab beetle and the Udjat – meaning healthy or sound – or Wedget eye of the sky god Horus. These were the amulet symbols most commonly depicted on Egyptian jewellery. The beetle represented Khepera, god of the morning sun, and was regarded as a symbol of immortality. The Udjat eye symbolised the eye lost by Horus, then restored and given to his father. Symbols of Tutankhamun's royal stature include the plaited beard and the sacred 'uraeus' (cobra) and vulture carved on his forehead. Another version of this pectoral is shown above.

Chinese Ritual Bronzes

Bronzeworking techniques were more highly developed in China than in any other ancient civilisation. The craft became established in about 1500 BC, during the Shang (Zhang) Dynasty, which ruled from 1766–1122 BC. Shang craftsmen produced a range of magnificent bronzes, including bells and even polished mirrors. The most impressive were ritual bronze vessels cast for the ancestor cult of the king and feudal lords.

with their own special function. A food cauldron constructed with three or four legs was known as 'Ting'. Wild, domesticated and imaginary animals, including horses, water buffalo, rams, tigers, elephants, deer and dragons, were popular motifs on bronze vessels. Owls, parrots, fish and snakes were also depicted on certain items.

The Chou (Zhou) people overran the Shang and established a dynasty which lasted from 1027 to 249 BC. Their bronzes took the form of spouted vessels, stylised birds and everyday utensils such as ladles and spoons. This was the time of China's earliest written records, when Confucius (551–479 BC) set down his ideology.

In the last part of the Chou period, called the age of Warring States (475-222 BC), central authority collapsed completely. Changes can be seen in bronze work as early as the Middle Chou period, when ritual bronze vessels lost some of the magical intensity of their imagery. In the time of the Warring States, ornamental detail on the bronzes was heightened by the use of inlays of gold, silver and turquoise, and decoration began to take the form of narrative images such as hunting scenes and figures.

Shang and early Chou craftsmen were helped in their work by the high lead content in the bronzes. This reduced the melting point of the metal and improved the flow in casting; it also reduced the number of surface flaws, and the softness of high lead bronze allowed craftsmen to chisel finer detail on the articles.

Loyang, a city on the south bank of the Yellow River in China's Hunan province, was the Chou Dynasty capital. After its fall in 311 BC the dynasty collapsed, and bronze making lost its importance. Some associated rituals undoubtedly declined – but the prestige of a ruler was still associated with the possession of decorated cauldrons and bells.

ABOVE:

The Chou dragon's head shown here is inlaid with gold and silver and was made in about the year 771 BC. It is now in the British Museum.

The 'ho' or 'yu' type wine vessel shown here was made sometime between the 14th and 12th centuries BC and is typical of the complex designs of that period, with strange configurations of birds, animals and dragons.

During the Shang Dynasty bronze-workers belonged to secret societies, which have been a feature of Chinese social history since early times. Many of the vessels they produced were used for animal and human offerings in ritual sacrifices to ancestors. These vessels each had named shapes,

This bronze ritual wine vessel from the Shang Dynasty depicts a tiger and a man, their bodies decorated with motifs of snakes and dragons, images which relate to a fertility cult which existed at the time.

BRONZE

Copper was probably the first metal smelted by man, but it is soft and does not hold a sharp edge. It is also difficult to cast, as gas bubbles form easily. Copper ores, which contain 10 or 12 per cent tin, make a harder metal, bronze.

The finest early bronze urns and statues were made by the Mesopotamians, Anatolians (early Turks) and Chinese from about the 3rd millennium BC. In archaeological terms, the Bronze Age occurred between the Stone and Iron Ages but its specific date varied from place to place.

The popularity of bronze came both from its enormous strength and from the fact that it is relatively easy to work. Its colour ranges from a dark silvery brown to a coppery red, depending mainly on how much tin is present. The surface of a bronze artefact may be enhanced by what is usually a green patina, which is caused by oxidation as it ages.

Olmec Figure Offerings

ABOVE:

The purpose of the snarling 'were-jaguar' jade figures isn't clear, but they may have been a type of rain god. This carving is now displayed at the American Museum of Natural History in New York.

RIGHT:

A Mexican jade mask pectoral or belt ornament.

The Olmecs founded the most ancient civilisation in Mexico, and probably in all of the New World. Besides growing tobacco and cotton, they collected rubber, hence the name Olmec which literally means 'rubber'. What is now central and southern Mexico, Guatemala and Honduras comprised the area known as Mesoamerica in which the Olmec settled; southern Veracruz and Tabasco has been referred to as their heartland, where the great Olmec sites were concentrated.

A group of 16 standing figures carved from serpentine and jade make up part of a spectacular burial offering at La Venta, the greatest Olmec ceremonial site. These are now housed in the National Museum of Anthropology in Mexico City. While only 6–7in (16–18cm) tall, the figures are simple but powerful, their faces marked by a highly distinctive snarl. La Venta in Tabasco, built between 800 and 300 BC on an island surrounded by mangrove swamps, features temple mounds of earth and large stone sculptures of heads with characteristic thick lips and heavy features, wearing what look like helmets.

The Olmecs were the first people of Mesoamerica to produce sculptures from large masses of stone. Some of their colossal carved heads weigh as much as 20 tonnes, and had to be brought to La Venta by water transport from mountains about 50 miles (80km) to the west. The centre was under the control of powerful priest-rulers who could command the labour needed for such projects.

Another example of their carving can be seen in jade figures called 'were-jaguars'. These combined the features of puffy-faced babies, often with a cleft at the top of the head, and fierce jaguars. The Olmecs believed that a woman cohabiting with a jaguar gave rise to this race of monsters.

The discovery of Olmec treasures dates

mainly from the 1930s and 1940s, when Matthew Stirling explored the sites of Tres Zopotes, La Venta and San Lorenzo. Archaeologists were led to the great treasures of San Lorenzo by following the gaze of a stone eye looking upwards from a trail. Patient excavation revealed a number of colossal heads carved from stone and small jade figurines.

The small figures in Olmec art are sculpted mainly from serpentine and jadeite and usually depict men with thick necks. The lower part of the faces is broad, with heavy jowls and a thin chin. The eyes are sometimes almond-shaped or simply take the form of narrow slits between heavy eyelids. The most distinctive feature is the large trapezoidal mouth with corners drawn downwards and a thick, flaring upper lip. The discovery of similar figures as far to the south-east as El Salvador suggests that Olmec control was widespread.

LEFT:
La Venta jade figurines are typical of Olmec carving. The arms and legs tend to be short and the figures are clad only in a loincloth.

SYMBOL OF THE JAGUAR

The image of the jaguar-god, which was worshipped by various cultures of pre-Columbian America, occurred especially frequently in the art of the Olmec and the Chavin of Peru. The Monte Alban Treasure, discovered in southern Mexico, included a Mixtec pectoral with a deity wearing a jaguar headdress. The jaguar's symbolism is powerfully presented but not always clear. Sometimes he appears as a rain god, while at other times he seems to be associated with sorcery or with royalty. In Aztec and Toltec Mexico the jaguar was the emblem of the warrior class, an idea which may derive from ancient China, where the jaguar also features.

Etruscan Gold Fibula

Etruscan civilisation flourished from about the 7th to the 3rd centuries BC in what is now central Italy, in the area between the rivers Arno and Tiber that was then known as Etruria. At its height Etruria controlled much of the Italian peninsula and its culture was highly sophisticated.

The origin of the Etruscans is uncertain, but it is thought they came from Asia Minor. Their great ability as metalworkers is displayed in the serpentine fibula shown, now in the British Museum; its rich parade of animals is hollow and weighs only a little more than 1oz (28g). Fibulas started as simple pins for fastening a cloak and gradually became much more elaborate objects which offered an opportunity for the display of Etruscan decorative skills. The earliest forms of fibula had no catch at the back but were simply held by passing the pin twice through the fabric and then bending it upward behind the head to secure it.

Another fibula, from the Bernardini Tomb – and now in the Museo Nazionale di Villa Giulia in Rome – shows the Etruscans' special mastery of granulation techniques (see panel). The decoration includes tiny gold lions, sphinxes and griffins.

Etruscan jewellery is generally divided into two phases. The finest and most delicate pieces were made during the early period, the 7th–5th centuries BC, using granulation. In the late Etruscan period, the 4th–3rd centuries BC, the

RIGHT:

This serpentine fibula from the Bernardini tomb shows the Etruscan genius for metalworking. Early patterns used granulation along the sides and terminals, and later versions added three-dimensional animal figures.

INSET:

Detail of the Bernardini Tomb fibula showing how skilfully the Etruscans controlled granulation techniques.

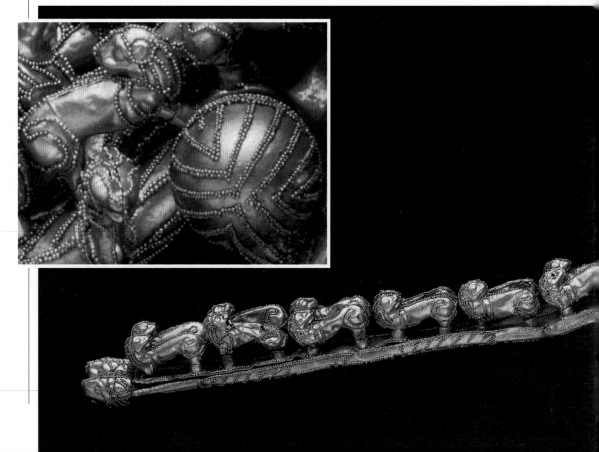

pieces produced were coarser in quality. In about 250 BC Etruscan civilisation was absorbed into the expanding Roman Empire, but the Romans continued to employ Etruscan goldsmiths for much of their work.

In the late 1820s a Roman goldsmith named Fortunato Pio Castellani became fascinated by Etruscan jewellery and tried to reproduce the style. He located some jewellers in Umbria who, as he thought, had preserved the ancient techniques, and brought them to Rome. While he never succeeded in precisely reproducing Etruscan jewellery, his imitations became world famous. When Castellani retired in the early 1850s, his sons extended the range of their 'archaeological' jewellery to include other ancient styles.

The Phoenicians, who lived at about the same time as the Etruscans, were renowned navigators who dominated trading around the Mediterranean from about 900 to 325 BC. As their trade routes developed, they set up new cities in Cyprus, Crete, Egypt, Sardinia, southern Spain and across North Africa in places such as Leptis Magna and Carthage.

Their travels established an important network for an interchange of ideas and artistic styles all over the ancient world. Phoenician jewellery from the 7th–6th centuries BC has been found in Tharros and Sardinia and also near Caceres, Spain. The gold bracelet shown here is from the Aliseda Treasure, uncovered in 1920 near Caceres. Much of what was found is now in the Museo Arqueológico Nacional in Madrid.

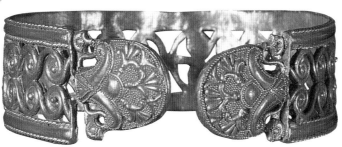

LEFT:

A Phoenician bracelet from the Aliseda Treasure displays granulation and filigree in openwork designs.

GRANULATION

Etruscans showed an unrivalled genius for the goldsmithing technique called 'granulation' in which tiny granules of gold, some measuring less than 0.005in (0.12mm), were used as decoration. Later goldsmiths found either that solder flowed between the granules, clogging the design, or that the granules themselves melted. It was not until 1933 that an English metallurgist, H A P Litterdale, developed 'colloidal hard soldering' which produced results remarkably similar to Etruscan granulation. This technique involves glueing the tiny granules to the background metal with a paste which becomes a solder when heated. The Etruscans must have been highly sophisticated metallurgists to have mastered a similar method in about 600 BC.

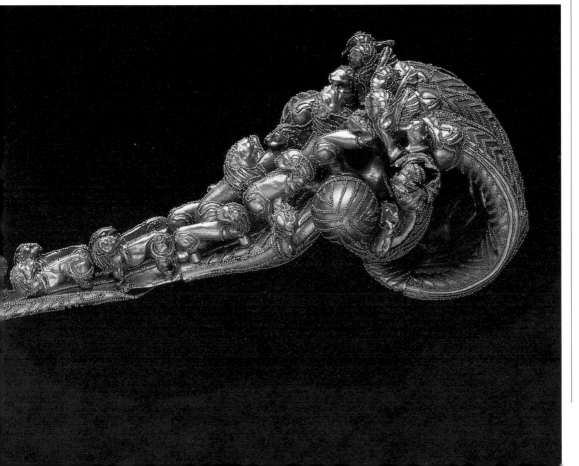

The Scythian Stag

A racing stag is characteristic of the energy displayed in work by Scythian craftsmen. Dating from the 6th–5th centuries BC, this gold animal plaque was found in what is now Hungary and is housed in the Budapest National Museum.

The Scythians emerged from nomadic obscurity in about the 7th century BC to control the area of Eastern Europe known as the Eurasian Steppes. As with other ancient people, it was traditional for Scythians to bury their dead with wealth and finery. Jewellery often included animal forms, such as boars, wolves, birds of prey and mythical beasts. Repoussé plaques were placed on the clothing of the corpse, and ornaments worn

RIGHT:

The dynamic pose of the Scythian stag is typical of the 'animal style' characteristic of this ancient metalwork.

OPPOSITE, ABOVE:

In the Oxus Treasure chariot the dress of the passengers is shown in great detail while finely drawn gold wire serves as a harness for the horses. The item may have been a votive temple offering.

OPPOSITE, BELOW:

Lively human action is reflected in the energetic style of the Chertomlyk Burial objects: the Scythian comb shown here depicts warriors.

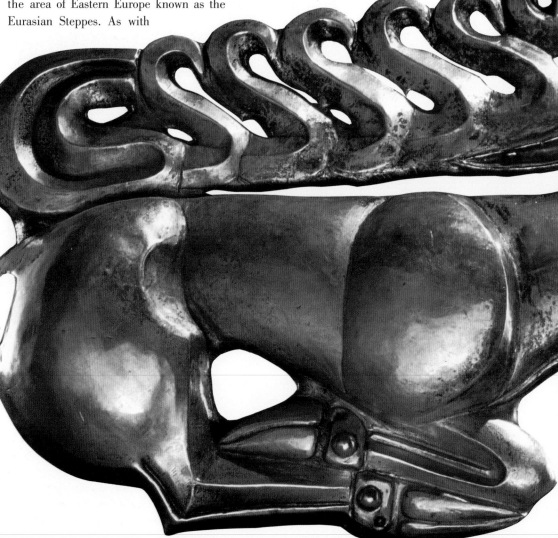

by the horses of a dead man were buried along with his body.

North of the Black Sea is an outstanding Scythian gravesite known as the Chertomlyk Burial. The 60ft- (18m-) high burial mound, dating from the 4th century BC, was found to contain several chambers holding the skeletons of a chieftain, his attendants and horses – as well as a remarkable hoard of precious objects. The fine gold and silver antiquities, showing a blend of Greek, Persian and Scythian styles, are now housed at the Hermitage Museum in Sankt-Peterburg (St Petersburg, formerly Leningrad).

While the main chamber of the

Chertomlyk Burial had been plundered, several side chambers were found to be virtually undisturbed. Besides gold rings and earrings, there were 400 gold strips depicting various animals and mythical monsters and a gold torque decorated with lions.

Another important hoard of Scythian jewellery is the Nymphaeum Treasure, which consists of Scythian jewellery, silver and bronze objects and pottery, found in the Crimea in 1868. It includes an unusual necklace of 22 rosettes with suspended acorns and lotuses, all made of sheet gold edged with beaded gold wire. This item can now be seen at the Ashmoleum Museum in Oxford.

In the 4th century BC the Sarmatians, who occupied territory to the east of the Scythians, increased their strength, defeated the Scythians and became dominant in the Eurasian Steppes for the next hundred years. One of the masterpieces of Sarmatian craftsmanship is a miniature gold chariot drawn by four horses. Dating from sometime in the 5th–4th centuries BC, the chariot contains a standing charioteer and a seated figure. It forms part of the Oxus Treasure, which was found in 1877 on a bank of the Oxus River (now the Amudarya River) in the Kataghan province of Afghanistan. The chariot and other artefacts from the Oxus Treasure are now housed in the British Museum in London.

THE HERMITAGE MUSEUM

When Catherine the Great came to the throne in 1762 she transformed the Winter Palace in St Petersburg into a retreat which she called the Hermitage. It opened as a court museum in 1764 and to the general public in 1852. It is now one of the most impressive museums in the world. In addition to its magnificent Scythian and Sarmatian metalwork collections, it has over 2,500,000 antiquities of interest.

Persian Silver Rhyton

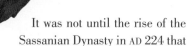

OPPOSITE:

A Persian silver drinking horn depicting a griffin, from 700–500 BC.

RIGHT:

A gold deer rhyton from the Panagjurist treasure.

BELOW:

This silver rhyton in the shape of a calf formed part of a funerary treasure found at Rozovec in Turkey. Like the gold deer, it is displayed in the Archaeological Museum, Sofia.

Persian civilisation was one of the most remarkable in the ancient world. It first became established on the Iranian plateau to the east of Mesopotamia in the 2nd millennium BC and evolved to build great cities and roads. The first major period of Persian art began with Cyrus the Great in the 6th century BC. The Archaemedians, as the region's inhabitants were called, used a wide variety of animals – from winged bulls to swans and ibexes – in their art. This is evident from vessels found at a number of important archaeological sites.

'Rhytons' are a distinctly Iranian type of drinking horn, usually moulded in the form of an animal such as a wolf, horse, ram, snake, griffin or stag. The Persian griffin horn illustrated is made in silver with gold foil and dates from the 5th century BC, about the time that the Archaemedians suffered a major defeat by the Greeks. When Alexander the Great delivered the final blow in 331 BC, he seized priceless treasures from the defeated Archaemedians. Some of these, deposited at Ecbatana (now Hamadan), were found earlier this century washed up by a flood. Among them were rhytons, fine gold bowls, gold swords and golden belt buckles in the form of two-headed lions, an important discovery which has collectively become known as the Hamadan Treasure.

It was not until the rise of the Sassanian Dynasty in AD 224 that Persia achieved another great artistic flowering. Jewellery of this period includes gold articles with pierced designs of monsters, birds, horses and hunting scenes. Silverware reflects the magnificence of life at court: plates, bowls, drinking vessels, jugs and ewers portray banqueting scenes, and on one jug musicians and tumblers perform while dancing girls display their charms.

The image of the enthroned king was a recurring theme among Sassanian gold and silver engravers. Two winged horses supporting the throne symbolised the immortality of the king's soul. Sassanian art glorified the monarch in the way that Byzantine art glorified Christ. The enthroned Sassanian king was seen as a divine being on earth.

Besides conventional animals, the Persians used imaginative, composite creatures in their decorations. The 'simurgh' mixes the forms of a peacock, lion, griffin and dog. According to legend, this is a mythical bird of good omen.

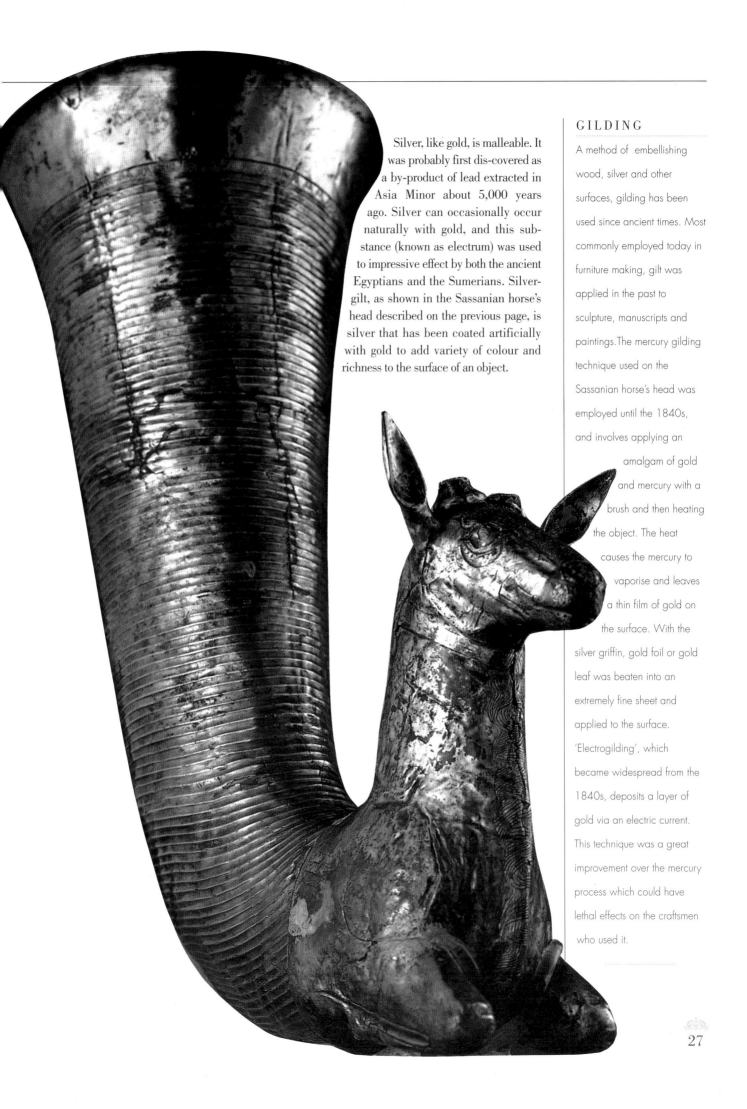

Silver, like gold, is malleable. It was probably first dis-covered as a by-product of lead extracted in Asia Minor about 5,000 years ago. Silver can occasionally occur naturally with gold, and this substance (known as electrum) was used to impressive effect by both the ancient Egyptians and the Sumerians. Silver-gilt, as shown in the Sassanian horse's head described on the previous page, is silver that has been coated artificially with gold to add variety of colour and richness to the surface of an object.

GILDING

A method of embellishing wood, silver and other surfaces, gilding has been used since ancient times. Most commonly employed today in furniture making, gilt was applied in the past to sculpture, manuscripts and paintings. The mercury gilding technique used on the Sassanian horse's head was employed until the 1840s, and involves applying an amalgam of gold and mercury with a brush and then heating the object. The heat causes the mercury to vaporise and leaves a thin film of gold on the surface. With the silver griffin, gold foil or gold leaf was beaten into an extremely fine sheet and applied to the surface. 'Electrogilding', which became widespread from the 1840s, deposits a layer of gold via an electric current. This technique was a great improvement over the mercury process which could have lethal effects on the craftsmen who used it.

Hellenistic Necklace

n Classical times (from 475 BC) Greece comprised a number of self-governing city-states, but these were united under Philip, King of Macedonia, in the early 4th century BC. His son, Alexander the Great, took control in 336 BC and established an empire over Asia Minor, Syria, Egypt, Mesopotamia, Persia, Afghanistan and the Indus

Bead necklaces of Classical Greece showed human heads, detail above; Hellenistic beads used more geometric patterns, detail right.

Valley. The period from the death of Alexander in 323 BC (the end of the Classical era) until the Roman conquest of Greece in 27 BC is now known as the Hellenistic Age.

Two important developments of that time were the spread of Greek culture into Egypt and Asia and a growing influence in Greece of oriental and Egyptian ideas. The Greek empire both absorbed decorative forms from other cultures and passed

its own ideas on to them. The metalwork produced in this era displays a rich hybrid of styles and influences as well as the importation of a number of new motifs, such as birds and the crescent.

Jewellery was no longer the sole preserve of royalty and the nobility and many pieces were produced for the new rich merchant class. While in Classical Greece gold was limited to domestic supplies, its availability increased greatly in Hellenistic times as a result of access to deposits in parts of Asia and Egypt.

Styles of jewellery, notably earrings, changed markedly: the boat-shaped earrings popular in Classical times had almost disappeared by the 2nd century BC, to be replaced by the hoop variety, made from twisted gold wires or hollow gold tubes. These came to a point at one end and had a finial at the other which was decorated with animal images, such as lions, goats, dogs and bulls. The gold necklace illustrated, from the 3rd century BC, has a repeating pattern of hollow beads. It is now in the British Museum, along with the other examples of jewellery shown here. The diadem is inlaid with cornelians and the 'Knot of Hercules'. This reef knot, another motif introduced into Hellenistic jewellery, was often combined with enamelling and filigree work.

An important innovation in Hellenistic Greece was the use of colour. Stones rarely appeared in the metalwork of Classical Greece but Hellenistic items show widespread use of cornelians, garnets, emeralds and amethysts, along with faience and enamels. There is also much fine filigree work and granulation, in the earrings especially.

As in Babylonia, Egypt and the Minoan and Mycenaean civilisations, engraved seals were used in Greece for identification and authenticity. Alexander the Great allowed only one artist to engrave his portrait on a gem and this then became the official seal. All of Alexander's rings served specific purposes connected with administration, and, when transferring his authority, the dying king gave his signet ring to his great general Perdiccas, to symbolise the transference of military power. Following Alexander's death, the vast empire he had built up was divided into smaller units.

ABOVE:
Part of a Hellenistic diadem showing the 'Knot of Hercules' motif, a talisman for healing, probably imported from Egypt.

LEFT:
A typical Hellenistic necklace of 330–200 BC.

FAIENCE

Hellenistic Greece absorbed much from Egyptian culture, including the use of a decorative material known as Egyptian faience (unrelated to ceramic faience) to make artificial gemstones. The process was devised by the Egyptians in order to solve the problem of a shortage of real stones, especially lapis lazuli. A mixture of ground quartz and blue copper compounds was heated in a blast furnace until fused into a lump which could then be cut and polished for inlay work.

Gundestrup Cauldron

A great silver-plated copper cauldron was discovered in a peat bog at Gundestrup in northern Denmark in 1891. With a diameter of over 27in (68cms), the cauldron is ornamented with relief decorations which offer intriguing clues concerning the religion of Celtic people living in the 2nd–1st centuries BC. The somewhat abstract and asymmetrical configurations on the surface are very typical of Celtic design. After a battle the spoils of victory were often thrown into bogs as a ritual thanks to the gods, and

RIGHT:
The Gundestrup Cauldron, showing an enlarged detail. In its entirety, the cauldron expresses the importance of the Celtic horse and rider, and provides the clearest images on record of an ancient Celtic army.

OPPOSITE, ABOVE:
The bronze face and binding of a Celtic shield which was probably made of wood and is known today as the Battersea Shield.

OPPOSITE, BELOW:
Gold torques were an important part of Celtic culture. Some have a very precise metal content and may have been used as currency jewellery.

priceless antiquities like the cauldron have been well preserved in this way. The cauldron is now housed at Copenhagen's National Museum.

The cauldron also gives an idea of the appearance of ancient Celtic warriors as they went into battle. Celts were known for their horsemanship, and the horsemen depicted on the cauldron wear short, tight-fitting linen tunics and iron helmets; lines of foot soldiers, armed with spears and shields but wearing no helmets, are followed by others blowing long trumpets shaped like horses' heads.

The Celtic peoples were a group of Indo-European tribes who probably evolved from the Battle-Axe culture of southern Russian in the 3rd millennium BC. By the early 2nd millennium BC, the Celts had spread widely over Western Europe but maintained common languages, customs and artistic styles.

A site in western Switzerland, La Tène, yielded many decorative Celtic metal objects of the 5th to 1st centuries BC when it was excavated in 1857. Adorned with flowing, interwoven tendrils and a range of animal forms, they match the decoration on artefacts found in countries as far afield as Britain and Ireland, showing how extensively Celtic cultures had spread. While the La Tène hoard was the largest find of immediate pre-Roman Celtic objects, other remarkable items have also come to light. One such individual treasure is the Battersea Shield, dredged from the River Thames at Battersea in London. Dating from the 1st century BC, it is a bronze Celtic shield nearly 3ft (91cm) high with embossed decoration and red enamel studs. The tendril ornamentation is highly characteristic

of Celtic work and is similar to that found on swords discovered at La Tène. The shield is now displayed at the British Museum in London.

The torque shown here, now in the National Museum of Ireland in Dublin, is a typical Celtic armlet, its terminals ornamented with engraving and relief work. While torques were generally worn by Celtic warriors, examples have also been found in graves of women and girls. Solid gold collars (also known as torques) made from sheets of beaten gold, usually decorated with small, stamped geometric motifs, were worn around the neck by both sexes.

THE VIX AND HOCHDORF TREASURES

The remarkable Celtic tomb of a young woman who had died in about 480 BC was discovered in France in 1929 at Vix, near Châtillon-sur-Seine. Undoubtedly a princess, she was adorned with amber beads, bronze ankle rings and fibulas with coral studs, and was buried in a small wagon.

Around her neck was a massive torque made from 17oz (480g) of pure gold. It comprised about 20 individual pieces and little winged horses on filigree and beaded threads. These winged horses have been found in other burials, such as the tomb in Hochdorf, near Stuttgart in Germany, where a prince was buried between 540 and 520 BC.

Chinese Jade Funerary Suit

When archaeologists uncovered and entered the massive tombs of Prince Liu Sheng and his wife Ton Wan in 1968, they were overwhelmed by the treasure they found. More than 2,800 articles had been buried along with the Prince in 113 BC, including many rare items of great beauty. As the elder brother of the Han Dynasty emperor Wu Ti, Prince Liu Sheng was important enough for the tombs to be cut deep into mountain rock and then blocked with stones before being sealed with molten iron. This iron wall had to be blown up with dynamite in order to allow the burial objects in the tombs to be recovered.

Each tomb was found to have several interconnecting chambers and even a room for bathing. The most remarkable discoveries were jade funerary suits (now held in Peking's Imperial Museum) that had enclosed the bodies of Liu Sheng and Ton Wan. Ancient Chinese texts describe how these jade cases were made for the bodies of Han emperors and high-ranking aristocrats, but those of Liu Sheng and his wife were the first ever found.

The Prince's amazing suit comprised 2,690 pieces of jade sewn together with 39oz (1,110g) of gold thread. The jade had been cut so that the

BELOW RIGHT:

It was thought that jade suits like those worn by Prince Liu Sheng and his wife contained magical powers that would preserve bodies. However, within their exquisite armour the royal couple had turned to dust and their funerary suits looked like piles of loose jade. Dummies were inserted to show how the suits had once fitted their wealthy owners. The inset shows a detail from the funeral suit of Princess Ton Wan.

OPPOSITE, ABOVE:

Unusual items in the tomb, and now in Beijing's Imperial Museum, were gilded bronze leopards with bright red garnets for eyes and silver circles to highlight the spots on their coats.

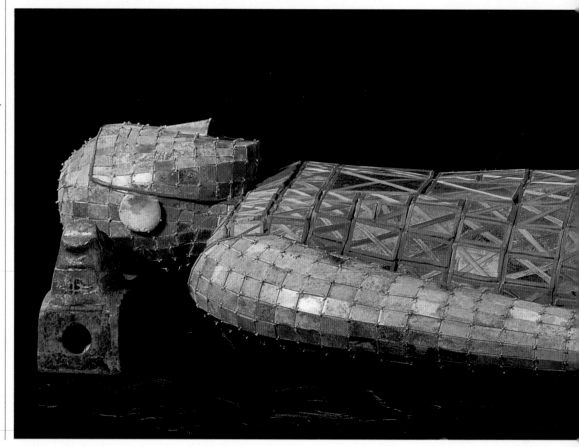

pieces fitted neatly together to make an armour-like shell. Holes had been drilled in the corners of every jade square, through which the gold wire could be threaded. As jade is a hard substance, requiring great skill to carve, an experienced craftsman must have laboured over ten years on just one of these suits.

Many other unusual objects were recovered from the tombs, including bronzes inlaid with gold, lacquerware, stone carvings and pottery figurines. In one chamber were several full-sized chariots with the remains of a dozen horses that had been buried along with the Prince. Tombs of this size and complexity must have required the work of

hundreds of men in all over several years.

What is known simply as 'jade' actually includes a variety of similar stones, the most important being nephrite and jadeite. The Chinese refer to an almost transparent green variety of jadeite as 'imperial jade'. Important religious symbols carved in jade include the Chinese 'pi', a pierced ring of jade symbolising heaven. Such pendants are often placed on coffins to help the deceased ascend to heaven.

Other cultures also value jade highly: the Maoris of New Zealand use it for ornaments and weapons and for carving Tikis – religious jade pendants in the form of an ancestor, sometimes with eyes made of mother-of-pearl.

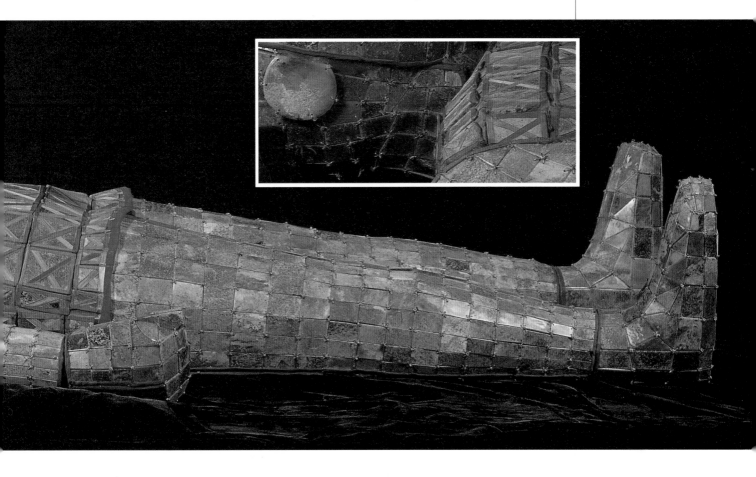

Hildesheim Wine Bowl

A rich collection of about 70 pieces of Roman silver dating from early in the 1st century AD was discovered near Hildesheim, Germany, in 1868. One of the most impressive vessels was a 'wine mixing bowl' (the ancients rarely drank their wine neat), decorated with naked children balancing on water plants which grow in winding curves around a pair of griffins. Some of the children are attacking crabs and eels with harpoons, while others are dragging animals from the water.

Besides this bowl, other notable finds in the hoard included three platters ornamented with figures of Minerva, Cybele and Hercules, and a silver folding tripod with detachable tray. The Hildesheim collection is now housed in the Staatliche Museum, Berlin.

Similar hoards of Roman vessels from the 1st century have been found at Pompeii, in southern Italy, which is itself one of the greatest archaeological treasures of the world. Before the eruption of Mt Vesuvius in August AD 79, Pompeii was a bustling Roman resort and commercial centre with a population of over 20,000. The remains of sumptuous villas and valuable antiquities show that it was a haven from Rome for wealthy citizens.

Over 20ft (6m) of volcanic ash covered the city after the eruption, and it was the late 1500s before Pompeii was finally rediscovered. Excavations began in earnest in 1748 and still continue today. By the 1970s over three-quarters of the city had been unearthed, revealing much about Greco-Roman art as well as Roman town-planning and architecture. Thousands of wall paintings and mosaics told stories of the everyday life of the people.

Another outstanding hoard of 118 silver items was found in the House of Menander, named after the Greek playwright who wrote comedies about the rich bourgeoisie. The house was owned by a wealthy family whose daughter married the Emperor Nero in AD 62. Items found there include the bowl shown here (left), which is also housed in the Staatliche Museum in Berlin. Another precious item from the same source was a round silver purse containing pieces of silver and gold.

The rich homes of Pompeii reflected the Roman ideal of enjoying the countryside while living in a town. Houses were built around a central courtyard containing a beautiful garden with statues and fountains. Frescoes in one house illustrated activities and occupations of the time, among them the work of a silversmith: a cupid is depicted busily making a piece of jewellery while

ABOVE:

This magnificent bowl is from a rich hoard of silver found at the House of Menander in Pompeii.

a pair of Roman scales and a smaller assay balance show how precious metals were weighed.

One of the most remarkable aspects of Pompeii is that animate figures as well as inanimate objects have been well preserved. Volcanic ash solidified around the bodies of humans and animals, making perfect ash moulds of their forms and even of the folds in their clothes. Plaster casts taken from these moulds now reproduce the attitudes of the desperate citizens of Pompeii as they tried to escape the burning ash.

THE BOSCOREALE TREASURE

In 1895 a man helping to excavate a large villa at Boscoreale, near Pompeii, uncovered a wonderful collection of silver at the bottom of an enormous wine vat. It is thought that a servant might have buried it there at the time of the Vesuvius eruption.

The Boscoreale collection, now in the Louvre in Paris, consists of 109 pieces, including a number of important items such as elaborate mirrors, drinking vessels and dishes. One of the most beautiful is a silver goblet with skeletons grouped in four separate scenes beneath garlands of roses. Each scene has an inscription which points out the moral it depicts, such as 'Enjoy life while ye may'.

ABOVE:
An exquisitely decorated bowl from the Hildesheim treasure.

LEFT:
A splendid Roman mixing bowl found near Hildesheim, Germany, which was used to dilute wine. The usual ratio was 8 gallons (36l) of water to 1 gallon (4.5l) of wine.

Roman Coin Rings

RIGHT AND OPPOSITE:

Coin rings, such as those illustrated here, were especially popular in Roman times.

BELOW:

Roman signet rings were highly functional, allowing the wearer to make a personalised impression in soft wax or clay.

For men and women of ancient Rome, rings were the most favoured items of jewellery. During the years before 27 BC the wearing of gold and the burial of gold articles were legally restricted. But these regulations were gradually relaxed and jewellery was plentiful during the time of the empire. As Roman rule expanded in the period from AD 200 to 400, new styles and techniques were developed. The wearing of several rings at the same time, as a practice common to both sexes, was introduced by the Romans, as was the adoption of rings as a sign of betrothal. The earliest Roman betrothal rings were made of iron since gold jewellery was so restricted, and they had no gemstone. While many rings were simply decorative, some also served useful functions as talismans and amulets, badges of office and seals of signature. The coin rings shown here include the head of Faustine, wife of Emperor Antoninus Pius (AD 138–61), and the profile of the Emperor himself; they are now in the British Museum, as is the seal ring illustrated.

Seals – devices for making an impression on a soft substance such as wax or clay – have been used since ancient times. They were often carved from cornelian, coral or other gemstones and mounted on gold signet rings. A document could therefore be authenticated by the wearer impressing his seal ring into hot sealing wax. Babylonian seals mainly took the form of engraved cylinders which were rolled to make an impression, while the Egyptians preferred stamping their seals. The Minoans in Crete gave great artistic importance to seals, which were usually worn around the neck or waist. The images they depicted varied widely, ranging from geometrical patterns to human and animal forms, ships, vases and letters.

In medieval times signet rings were used by messengers as credentials, to confirm their identity. Seals were often suspended from a neck chain in the 16th century and from a watch chain in the 17th century. By the 18th century signet rings had become less functional and were generally worn as decoration. Typical rings of the 19th century were simple gold bands adorned only with an intaglio initial or monogram.

Coins have long been incorporated into jewellery by a variety of cultures. Coin bracelets, dating from the early 17th century, in the form of a rigid gold hoop with a front ornament made of adjacent gold coins, have been found in Egypt, and a large number of coin pendants, often worn as amulets, have also been discovered. German coin pendants of the 16th and 17th centuries were usually presented as a gift to visiting dignitaries or favoured servants. Watch cases incorporating a coin were fashionable from the early 19th century, especially in France, where they were set with a 100-franc coin. The first coins used as official or generally recognised currency appeared around the Mediterranean region in the 1st millennium BC but 200 years earlier people were already weighing out and exchanging cut up and broken bits of

silver. Hoards of variously sized and shaped ingots, as well as scale pans and scale weights, have been found in a number of locations.

GOLD COINAGE

The first gold coins were probably produced by the Ancient Greeks in about 700 BC. Since then they have been minted all over the world.

Gold keeps its lustre and colour for ever, and coins that have been buried for 2,000 years have been discovered in the same untarnished condition as when they were hidden. Its rarity makes gold inherently precious, which is why it has remained a symbol of security in times of economic uncertainty.

Even relatively modern gold coins have a high scarcity value: when gold was discovered in Australia in the 1850s a few gold coins, stamped with a kangaroo and the mark of their 1-oz (28-g) weight, were privately produced; these are now highly prized.

The Triton Dish

A superb round silver dish with a heavily beaded rim was amongst a hoard unearthed at Mildenhall, Suffolk, in 1946. The collection consists of 34 silver objects found by a farmer while turning a field, with his plough set to work 4 inches (10cm) deeper than usual. Rich designs on the bowls and dishes were totally obscured by encrustation and were only revealed later by careful cleaning. A variety of coins amongst the hoard showed the faces of Roman emperors Honorius and Constantine III. These coins helped to date the Mildenhall Treasure to the 4th century.

A massive Roman force had invaded Britain in AD 43 and came to control the whole island south of Scotland. The occupying army built an impressive road system, introduced their arts and crafts techniques, and encouraged the inhabitants to build Roman-style towns and villas and to use Roman money.

The Triton Dish, illustrated here, is a flanged bowl 9 inches (23cm) in diameter. Riveted on to the apex of its roughly fitting domed lid is a cast figure of Triton blowing on a conch shell. The bowl is incised on the upper surface with a stylised running floral scroll. Among the many silver artefacts from the same source are a number of silver ladle handles in the form of stylised dolphins.

The Oceanus Dish, nearly 2 ft (61cm) in diameter, is covered with

RIGHT:
The silver Triton Dish, depicting Triton sitting atop the domed lid and centaurs battling against fearsome lions.

BELOW AND CENTRE:
The highly decorated silver bridal casket found on the Esquiline Hill in Rome is very similar to Roman objects found at Mildenhall, Suffolk.

THE BRITISH MUSEUM

Founded in 1753, the British Museum in Bloomsbury, London, is the oldest museum in the world. Its impressive collection of artefacts was started by the physician Sir Hans Sloane and now includes treasures covering two million years of world history and civilisation. They are displayed in over 94 galleries extending 2½ miles (4km). The main part of the present building dates from the mid-19th century. Room 40 contains the silver Mildenhall Treasure, along with a variety of other pieces dating back to the era of the Roman Empire.

A rich mixture of metallic and jewelled objects can be seen in the museum, including a table clock made for a Holy Roman Emperor in the form of a golden galleon, a number of medieval walrus-tusk chessmen from an island off the mainland of Scotland and a bronze cat with gold nose ring from Ancient Egypt.

figure reliefs; the central image is a mask of Oceanus with staring eyes, a broad nose and cheeks, a heavy moustache and seaweed beard, four dolphins frolicking between the wild locks of his hair. Then in two concentric rings around this image, separated by a border of scallop shells, is a series of vigorously depicted figurative scenes. These include Bacchus, the Roman god of wine, standing with his foot on the back of a panther and holding a bunch of grapes, and Hercules being saved from collapse by two helpful young satyrs; one buttresses him from the front while the other clasps him around the middle from behind. Figures from Roman mythology complete the circle around the bowl, playing musical instruments, leaping and dancing, the draperies of the women swirling gracefully around them.

The Mildenhall objects, which were either made in or were imported into Britain during the 400 years of Roman occupation, bear a resemblance to items from the treasure discovered on the Esquiline Hill in Rome in 1793. This hoard includes the highly decorated bridal casket shown here. Both the Oceanus Dish and the Esquiline Casket are now in the British Museum. Another important Roman hoard, also now in the British Museum, was found on a building site in Norfolk in 1979. Known as The Thetford Treasure, the find includes gold rings, necklaces, bracelets and a gold belt buckle, and is thought to have been part of a jeweller's stock.

The British Museum (see panel) is offered first refusal on any items discovered in Britain and deemed 'treasure-trove' by a coroner's inquest. This would almost inevitably apply to any large hoard that was not part of a burial. The finder is awarded the full market value of the find.

Crux
Vaticana

The 6th-century cross made of silver gilt and studded with jewels, opposite, was a gift from the Byzantine Emperor Justin II to the Vatican. The emeralds, hyacinths, alabaster, agates, aquamarines and jaspers with which it is inset were originally surrounded by a row of 16 large oriental pearls, but these are now missing. The splendid cross is the oldest object in the treasury of St Peter's in Rome.

With the rise in Christianity, crosses and crucifixes became increasingly important objects. Early crosses were small and made only of gold, but gradually gemstones were added and larger processional crosses introduced to give more dignity and colour to Church rituals. Gems, cut in flat, tabular fashion or as rounded cabochons, were placed in settings raised above the surface of the cross and held in place by prongs.

The gems that were used all had some religious significance as well as being decorative. Lapis lazuli symbolised truth and the hope of heaven, while green jasper stood for the constant renewal of faith. Red garnet was used to represent the blood of martyrs. A circle signified eternity and perfection, a square symbolised the world and those living within it and a triangle represented the Trinity. Ancient descriptions of St Peter's testify to the extraordinary wealth of its treasures and decorations, which were renewed by donations

OPPOSITE:

The 6th-century Crux Vaticana is one of the few early items left in the treasury of St Peter's in Rome.

RIGHT:

As he died before reaching his jubilee year, the Ceremonial Jubilee Hammer commissioned by Pope Paul III was passed to his successor, Julius III.

from emperors and votive offerings from pilgrims from all over the world. Many of these early items are now missing as St Peter's was pillaged repeatedly over the centuries. Others were lost to the Napoleanic armies in 1797 under the Treaty of Tolentino with Pope Pius VI. The remaining collection is sadly diminished, but it nonetheless comprises some fine items, such as the ring of Pope Sixtus IV and a 15th-century candelabra by Pollaiuolo.

One item related to St Peter's but now in the Bayerisches Nationalmuseum, Munich, is the Ceremonial Jubilee Hammer. This bears the arms of Pope Julius III and is a glorious example of Renaissance metalwork. The artistry is so fine that it has been attributed to the master goldsmith Cellini. Such richly decorated hammers were intended for use by the reigning Pope at the ceremonial opening of the doors of St Peter's during his jubilee year (jubileum) which occurred only every 25 years. The hammer shown was commissioned by Paul III, who was Pope from 1534 until his death in 1549. He did not live to use the hammer, which was then passed to the new Pope and the arms of Julius III were added.

Another great papal treasure is the Fisherman's Ring, a gold signet ring used to authenticate documents. A new ring is made for each new Pope, and the old ring is then destroyed.

PAPAL RINGS

Some papal rings are massive, too large to wear on any finger, and are made of gilded bronze, with a wide, heavy hoop and high, square bezel. Usually set with glass, crystal or some quite ordinary stone, they bear the arms of a Pope or cardinal on the bezel, together with papal symbols such as the triple crowns and crossed keys. Some dating from the 11th and 12th centuries have been found but most of those in existence date from the 1400s and 1500s. The purpose of these papal rings is not certain, but the frequency with which they have come to light suggests that they were not made exclusively for select high church officials – and were certainly not intended as jewellery for the Pope alone. They might have been carried by papal emissaries as a form of identification, and possibly even given as souvenirs by the Pope to visiting pilgrims.

The Byzantine Empress

In AD 330 the capital of the Roman Empire was formally transferred from Rome, its original seat, to Byzantium, on the shore of the Sea of Marmara. The city took its new name, Constantinople, from the Emperor Constantine. As the heart of the Roman Empire moved eastwards, the importance of Rome gradually diminished.

At the height of its power in the 6th century, the Byzantine Empire controlled a wide spread of territory – embracing Balkan lands stretching as far as the Danube and including the territories of Syria, Asia Minor, Egypt and Libya as well as the whole of Italy. Internal factions caused it to decline in the 11th century and it was finally overthrown by the Turks who captured Constantinople in 1453.

Constantine was the first Christian emperor, and the advent of Christianity profoundly affected artistic creations of all kinds. The tradition of burying the dead with fine jewels and metalwork was discouraged, and early Byzantine metalwork began to convey a strong religious sense.

The materials used were much the same as those employed in Roman art, but gold, precious and semiprecious stones and glass were combined in new ways, and the openwork technique of *opus interrasile* was developed and much improved. The art of Ravenna included some of the finest Byzantine creations, including sumptuous mosaics. A mosaic on the wall of the church of San Vitale in Ravenna shows the Emperor Justinian with his Empress Theodora and their retinue, all richly bejewelled.

The ivory carving of the Empress shown on the panel illustrated here displays the long earrings with several pendant strings that were typical of the time. Ivory was carved with great skill to depict intricate scenes on caskets and diptychs. These diptychs (carvings made in two compartments that are hinged side by side, and fold over each other to protect the decoration) varied enormously in size from large altarpieces to small pendants.

This image probably represents the Empress Ariadne, who died in 515. It has been suggested that it might alternatively portray the 6th-century Empress Constantina or the Empress Irene, which would date it to about 800. However, the style of

CORNELIANS AND OTHER CHALCEDONIES

Cornelians, as shown on the Byzantine earrings, are a variety of the quartz gemstone chalcedony. These semiprecious stones can range in colour from yellowish-red to reddish-brown, intensifying in tone if they are heated. Tough and hard, cornelians are often carved and used as seals or fashioned into beads. The name most likely derives from the Latin *cornum*, which means a cornelian cherry. Varieties of chalcedony include agate, sardonyx, sard, chrysoprase, onyx, prase and others. The stone is widely imitated by the use of coloured glass. After the late 1800s chalcedony was sometimes dyed black to take the place of jet, a variety of lignite or coal which could be carved and engraved; jet was used extensively in the 19th century for lockets and other jewellery associated with mourning.

the carving links it with others made in about the year 500. Besides being richly bejewelled, the Empress carries a sceptre and orb and sits in a recess topped by a dome, above which are eagles with chains in their beaks. This panel is now in the Kunsthistorisches Museum, Vienna.

The earrings illustrated, also from the 6th century and now in the Benaki Museum in Athens, are similar to those worn by the Empress in the carving illustrated opposite. Cloisonné enamelling was widely used at this time. Both men and women wore earrings and other jewels such as gold pendants and rings. Cuff bracelets, in the form of wide cylindrical bands tapering at one end, were another type of Byzantine jewellery. These bracelets were made of gold and then decorated with filigree and enamel work depicting animal images and abstract shapes.

ABOVE AND CENTRE:

The spaces between the tubes of the 6th-century Ålleberg Collar are decorated with small animals and cherubic faces cut from gold plates.

BELOW:

A fine example of a 9th-century brooch in gold with precious stones, from Ovre Eiker, Norway

VIKING JEWELLERY

The name Viking, from the Norse word *vik* , meaning bay or creek, was adopted by the Scandinavians in the 9th century to signify 'sea voyage'. The Vikings, who occupied much of Denmark, a large part of Norway and the south of Sweden, were highly skilled ironsmiths; large farms had their own forges and peasants often made their own requirements, extracting the raw iron ore from bogs. Gold and silver were also skilfully worked, as can be seen from these gold brooches, the twisted gold ring and the silver ring and necklace bearing a pendant in the form of Thor's hammer.

As ships lay at the very heart and soul of Viking life, it is not surprising that they were used as burial containers for the remains of important people, along with jewels, weapons and even kitchen utensils for use in another life. Many ship burial sites from the 7th century have been discovered at Valsgärde and Vendel in Sweden. The wrecks of five Danish ships discovered in the 1950s at the Fiord of Roskilde are now on view there at the purpose-built Viking Ship Museum.

THE ÅLLEBERG COLLAR

This beautiful rigid circular collar in fine gold dating from the 6th century was unearthed at Ålleberg, Sweden, and is now displayed at the Statens Historiska Museum in Stockholm. The entire surface of each of its three concentric tubes is decorated with rings, granulation and filigree work. This delicacy is also evident on rings of the time.

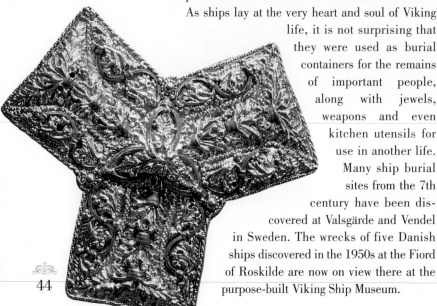

THE HEDEBY HOARD

Another important collection of Viking jewellery (again from a ship burial), the Hedeby Hoard, was dredged in 1979 from the mud of Hedeby harbour, located just south of the present German/Danish border.

As an important trading centre, Hedeby attracted a wide range of artisans who specialised in making pottery, glass, copper and bronze goods and fine amber jewellery. This particular hoard includes a gold and bronze pin, an amber ring, carved bone combs and a gold filigree earring, but its most interesting items were 40 bronze relief blanks over which pieces of metal were pressed to make gold and silver jewellery.

These articles, thought to date from about the year 1000, are now housed in the Schleswig-Holsteinisches Landesmuseum für Vor- und Frühgeschichte in Schleswig, Germany.

OSEBERG SHIP BURIAL

One of the most impressive Viking burials was excavated in 1904 in Vestfold. Dating from about AD 800, the hoard included a wagon, sledges, footwear, weaving equipment and even beds – all with carved motifs. More precious items such as jewellery were missing, presumably looted. The remains of two women were also found.

THE VENDEL HELMET

The Vendel helmet (top right) is now in the Upplandsmuseet in Uppsals, Sweden. The helmet is divided into rectangular panels, the lower part shaped from iron links. These items were produced by the forerunners of the Vikings. This particular example is known as Sigurd's Helmet, possibly referring to Sigebert of the Franks, who died in AD 575. The bronze visor and crest add to the helmet's fierce appearance. A similar example, also from the 7th century, is the Valsgärde helmet.

Sutton Hoo Shoulder Clasp

n 1939 one of the finest archaeological finds ever made in Britain was uncovered in a sandy barrow near Woodbridge, in Suffolk. Clustered there on a hill are fifteen large mounds, and the previous year the owner of the land had hired an amateur archaeologist to investigate. While most tombs within the mounds had been plundered in the past, careful excavation subsequently revealed an undisturbed grave deposit of great worth.

Known as the Sutton Hoo Burial, it comprised the regalia of a 7th-century Anglo-Saxon ruler. The Anglo-Saxons were Germanic people who inhabited and ruled England from the 5th century AD to the Norman Conquest in 1066. In both size and wealth, the riches of the Sutton Hoo Burial far exceeded those of every other Anglo-Saxon grave in England. The owner of the land was awarded the treasure, which she then generously donated to the British Museum in London.

One of the hoard's most remarkable pieces is a two-part hinged shoulder clasp with complex geometric designs picked out in red and blue cloisonné enamel (see panel). The two curved halves are fastened with a gold pin attached by a chain. There are 20 tiny separate squares of different enamels, creating an intricate chequerboard design. The shoulder clasp also incorporates a style of enamelling known as 'mock-champlevé'. This imitates real champlevé (see panel) which is a variation on cloisonné.

Another important piece from the treasure is the

ABOVE AND RIGHT:

The decoration on the Sutton Hoo shoulder clasp includes millefiori glass – coloured glass embedded in clear glass, usually in flower-like designs. This technique was used in Egypt in the 3rd century BC and in Rome in the 1st century AD; it was revived in Venice in the 16th century.

OPPOSITE:

Belt buckles with fine geometric designs, like this one from the Sutton Hoo Burial, were important items of male jewellery in the 6th and early 7th centuries.

The Sutton Hoo brooch uses the form of enamelling known as cloisonné, achieved by soldering a series of thin metal strips on to a metal surface to form a pattern. The resulting partitions, or 'cloisons', are then filled with coloured enamels and fired, and the surface is ground flat and polished. Gilding the exposed metal edges enhances the rich, jewel-like appearance of the object. The Mycenaeans first developed cloisonné enamelling in the 13th–11th centuries BC. By the 3rd century BC it was practised widely in Western Europe, and Celtic jewellers became especially proficient at the technique.

belonged to a king who had been baptised but had given up the faith. Raedwald fitted this picture exactly, as he was baptised a Christian but later reverted to his original pagan beliefs.

Besides fine gold jewels, the boat contained a sceptre, a gold purse (with 40 gold coins and two small ingots), silver bowls and plates, mounted silver drinking horns, bronze cauldrons and silver and gold ship fittings. Among a number of weapons

chased gold belt buckle illustrated here, which is decorated with niello, a black compound used to incise a design on metal (see page 71), and punctuated by three gold rivets.

The 80-ft (23.7-m) long, oar-driven burial ship was probably a monument to Raedwald, the last great pagan king of East Anglia who died in about 625. The boat itself may have come from eastern Sweden in the mid-6th century with a group who founded a dynasty in East Anglia. There was widespread conversion to Christianity in the 7th century and burials after that time tended to be in churches and churchyards. Two silver spoons in the Sutton Hoo Burial suggested the grave

were a shield with bronze and gilt decoration, a sword with a jewelled gold hilt and an iron helmet with bronze and silver fittings and 'eyebrows' edged in garnets.

Silla Bronze

Korean art and crafts reflect the country's geographical position at the meeting point of the Chinese Empire and the island kingdom of Japan. At the time of the powerful Chinese Han Empire, the peninsula that is now Korea was part of China. The Chinese were driven out of Korea in 313 and this initiated the Korean era of the Three Kingdoms (313–668).

Located in the south-east of Korea, Silla was the last of the Three Kingdoms to receive Buddhism (in 535). For nearly a thousand years its capital was a place called Kyŏngju which was founded in about 35 BC. Called the 'Golden City', it had flourished greatly to become one of the most splendid cities in the world by the 7th century.

Silla's population was organised into a complicated class system with the mass of people living in conditions of near slavery. Land ownership was entirely in the hands of the state. Uprisings by the peasants finally undermined the power of the Silla kingdom which then split into smaller states.

One example of fine treasure from the Silla kingdom is an early 7th-century gilt bronze called the Bodhisattva Maitreya. 'Bodhisattva' is a Buddhist term for spiritual beings incarnated as men. They act as powers of goodness by living amongst suffering humanity. While considered saintly, such beings, unlike the Buddha himself, are not divine. Its style was imitated in Japan, and many bronze items of this type have survived.

The gilt-bronze standing figure shown opposite, depicting the Buddha Amitabh, is another example of this type of image, but this time representative of the Unified Silla dynasty of the 8th century. This piece is now in the British Museum in London.

Besides their fine works in gold and bronze, people of the Old Silla period displayed a strong interest in astronomy. Existing evidence for this is provided by a 7th-century bottle-shaped observatory tower which supported instruments for studying the sky and stars.

In 1921 archaeologists discovered the Gold Crown Tomb at Kyŏngju, which contained an exciting array of grave treasures dating from the 5th to 7th centuries. The find is named after a splendid gold crown, which can now be seen on display in the Kyŏngju National Museum. It is characteristic of Korean goldworking, whose speciality was the use of thinly rolled gold foil and gold wire; few items were made of solid metal. It is probable that the crown was used only for ritual or funerary purposes, as it was covered by large numbers of small spangles. Such spangles were also found on other items in the treasure trove, including gilt bronze shoes.

The circlet of the crown supports fine upright projections enclosing an inner cap with antler-like branches. The outer structure is made of cut sheet gold ornamented with punched dots, and the whole crown is decorated with small jade pendants shaped like commas hung on lengths of twisted wire. Jade ornamentation similar to this also occurs in Japanese decorative art.

What appear to be antlers on the Silla crown may be a link to shamanist beliefs in the Old Silla period of the 5th and 6th centuries. Early rulers of the kingdom were a kind of priest-prince who took the title of king only in the 6th century.

RIGHT:
This Silla gilt bronze headdress ornament dates from the Koryo period of the 10th–14th centuries.

OPPOSITE:
The drapery on this 7th-century gilt bronze Bodhisattva is very like that of northern Chinese sculpture. This is not surprising as Korean nobles and monks went to China to study and Chinese influence on the arts in Silla was considerable.

SHAMAN'S CHARMS

The Korean shamanistic crown is one of many treasures from different cultures that may have had magical connections. In Alaska, Eskimo shamen (medicine men) wore charms that represented the spirit being called to capture the soul of the intended victim. In Alaska and British Columbia such pieces were carved of walrus ivory or the horn of moose or reindeer with decorations of abalone shell. A number of these can be seen in the Museum of the American Indian (Heye Foundation) in New York.

Any object worn or carried for its supposed power to bring good fortune or ward off illness or evil can be defined as a charm. The Korean crown is hung with jade pendants to bring good luck, but charms in other societies have taken many forms. Small gold animals, horseshoes, four-leaf clovers, hearts and even signs of the zodiac have been worn on charm bracelets since the early 19th century.

Sun Lord Pacal of Palenque

The Mayan Indians of Central America created a highly organised civilisation that lasted approximately from 300 BC to AD 1500. At the height of their power they controlled a vast area, stretching from north-west Honduras through most of Guatemala to the southern Mexican states. Each Mayan city had its own ruler and a cere-monial centre for worshipping gods. Most people were humble farmers who were also employed as labourers to build ritual structures for the powerful priestly class. Religion permeated all aspects of Mayan life.

RIGHT AND BELOW:
An 8th-century Mayan jade plaque featuring a noble and a clown of the court. There were strongly marked classes in Mayan society, with nobles owning private lands and holding political office.

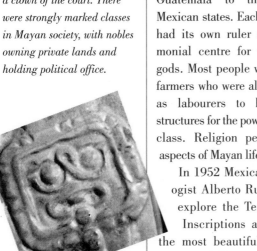

In 1952 Mexican archaeol-ogist Alberto Ruz set out to explore the Temple of the Inscriptions at Palenque, the most beautiful of all the centres of Mayan civilisation. The site lies at the foot of a chain of low hills covered with tall rainforest. On remov-ing a stone from the temple, Ruz hit upon a vaulted stairway leading into the interior of a stone pyramid. After removing numerous obstacles he displaced a slab and discovered a great funerary crypt. Inside it a Mayan ruler had been put to rest with a treasure trove of jade. A mosaic mask of jade, the eyes made of shell and obsidian, covered the face (this is now in the American Museum of Natural History, New York); necklaces of jade covered the chest and jade rings adorned the fingers; a large piece of jade was placed in each hand and another in the mouth. This was the tomb of Sun Lord Pacal who took the throne at the age of

12 and died in 683 at 80. He had built the crypt to hold his remains in the same way as pyramids were built for the Egyptian pharaohs.

Over the sarcophagus of Sun Lord Pacal was a slab of stone carved in low relief. The Mayans excelled in this low-relief carving, producing fine plaques in both stone and jade. The thin jade plaque shown here, from Nebaj, Guatemala, dates from about AD 750 and shows a richly dressed noble talking with a dwarf servant. The plaque is now in La Aurora Museum, Guatemala City.

While no commoner would have been buried like Sun Lord Pacal, jade played a part in all burials. Ordinary folk would have been buried beneath the floors of their homes, their mouths filled with food and a single jade bead. Items they had used while they were alive were buried with them. Death was dreaded by nobles and commoners alike, as there was no automatic path to any paradise.

In the 9th or 10th century Mayan civilisation collapsed abruptly and many religious centres were abandoned. By the time the Spanish conquerors arrived in the mid-16th century, what had been a great Mayan empire consisted of little more than weak chiefdoms. There are still over six million Mayan people in Central America today, but – like many other groups of Indians – their traditional lifestyle has been diminished by outside influences.

TREASURE AT CHICHÉN ITZÁ

In the early 1900s a hoard of Mayan jewellery was recovered in the Yucatan area of Mexico by Edward H. Thompson when he dredged an important ceremonial well at Chichén Itzá, into which offerings to the rain god had regularly been thrown. The Well of Sacrifice, as the site was called, contained a wealth of gold jewellery, mostly imported from Panama and Costa Rica, and large numbers of locally made items in jade. As well as appeasing the gods with treasures, it was customary to try and win their help by sacrificing live humans in times of drought.

LEFT:
The 7th-century jade mask of Sun Lord Pacal was meant to protect the ruler. The word 'jade' derives from the Spanish piedra de ijada, *the name given to the stone by the Spaniards (who believed it could ease kidney pains) in the 16th century.*

Ardagh Chalice

*O*ne of the finest surviving artefacts of the Celtic Church in Ireland is the early 8th-century Ardagh Chalice, made of beaten silver with areas of gilt. The chalice was found in 1868 by a boy digging potatoes south of the Shannon estuary. The object lay concealed under a stone slab between the roots of a thorn bush, along with four brooches and a small bronze chalice. The treasures are now in the National Museum of Ireland in Dublin.

There was widespread conversion to Christianity in Ireland in the 5th century, and for the next three centuries the country was the most important centre of Christianity in north-west Europe. Glittering chalices and book covers brightened many early churches but, regrettably, the Ardagh Chalice is one of the few items to have survived virtually intact.

Its design is enhanced by an intricate and typically Celtic pattern in gold wire punctuated by red and blue studs, but much of the soft silver surface of the chalice is left undecorated, which adds to its great elegance. The red and blue studs

BELOW:

The early 8th-century Ardagh Chalice contrasts large areas of plain silver with glittering studs and delicate gold wire filigree.

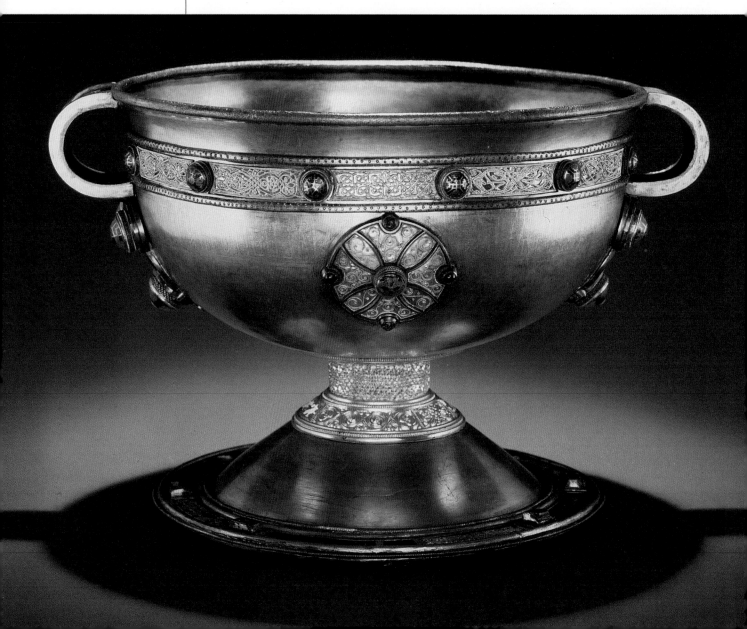

are similar to those on brooches and other objects made at that time. The opaque red enamel contrasts well with the blue glass which reflects the light. The Tara Brooch, which was discovered at Bettystown, County Meath, and was made at about the same date, also has red and blue studs as well as raised amber beads. The fierce-looking reptiles on the brooch are typical of animal motifs often used at that time. Human forms were hardly ever portrayed.

Another piece of treasure found near Limerick was the Shannongrove Gorget, which is now in the Victoria and Albert Museum. This was made much earlier than the chalice and dates from the Irish Bronze Age – about the 7th century BC. The gorget, a woman's collar, is made of thin gold and decorated with concentric repoussé ribbing. At each end is a circular cupped terminal, also with concentric ribbing.

The great glory of Ireland's Late Bronze Age is its goldwork, and some astounding collections have been recovered. Among them is the great Clare find, a hoard of 146 gold objects found in County Clare when a narrow-gauge railway was being constructed in 1854. Many of the pieces were melted down, but casts were made first and are now displayed in the National Museum in Dublin.

A large proportion of Ireland's rich gold ornaments of the 8th and 7th centuries BC has come from counties bordering the lower reaches of the River Shannon. The fact that so much has been found in bogs or close to water suggests that precious objects may have been thrown into water to appease the gods.

The 7th-century BC Shannongrove Gorget is a fine example of goldwork from pre-Christian Ireland.

Remains of Celtic jewellery have also been found in Scotland. The Hunterston Brooch is an early 8th-century Scottish Celtic silver pin brooch, whose ornament includes interlaced gold filigree and cells set with amber. Now in the National Museum of Antiquities in Edinburgh, the brooch was found in 1826 on the estate of Robert Hunter in Ayrshire (now Strathclyde).

BELOW:
The early 8th-century Hunterston Brooch shows traditional Celtic design work and the use of amber decoration.

AMBER

Amber has been popular since the Bronze Age in cultures ranging from Tibet and Mongolia to Ethiopia and Morocco, as well as in Celtic Britain. It is not a true gemstone but rather a fossilized natural resin from an extinct type of pine tree. The colour of amber can vary widely, and pieces showing two colours have sometimes been cut as cameos. The two main varieties are sea amber and pit amber and, while amber is soft, it is tough and can be intricately carved.

One of the world's most remarkable treasures was the Amber Room of Tsarskoe Selo: over 55 sq yds (5 sq m) of carved amber panels backed with silver foil, made in about 1709 for Frederick I of Prussia. These were taken from the Summer Palace outside St Petersburg in 1942 and have since disappeared.

The Golden Buddha of Bangkok

OPPOSITE:

This 10ft- (3m-) high Golden Buddha was disguised in stucco to conceal its true worth. It is now in the Wat Traimit temple in Bangkok.

RIGHT:

Sri Lanka's relic of the Buddha's tooth, a copper bas relief, is the nation's most prized possession and has become a symbol of sovereignty.

When a construction company extended the Thai port of Bangkok earlier this century it unearthed a massive Buddha statue covered in stucco. On the night before the figure was due to be moved, torrential rains soaked and loosened the outer casing. During transportation the next day, the Buddha was dropped into mud which caused the stucco to crack. The accident was fortuitous as it revealed the true magnificence of the object within. Experts think the statue, a temple sculpture, was covered to conceal its 5½ tonnes of gold from the invading Burmese army in the 18th century.

Another remarkable Buddhist image in Bangkok is the giant reclining Buddha at an old temple called Wat Phra Jetupon. This is Thailand's largest Buddha, an incredible 150ft (46m) long and 50ft (15m) high. It is covered entirely with gold leaf and the soles of the feet are inlaid with designs in mother-of-pearl.

About half of the world's population embraces Buddhism, and the movement has affected nearly every part of Asia. From its Indian homeland, about 2,500 years ago, Buddhism has evolved into different forms. While the founder of Buddhism was against the making of images and the possession of material goods, the Buddhist religion has acquired a wealth of objects for veneration. Until the 1st century AD Buddhist art never portrayed the Buddha himself but only symbols that represented his teachings. Besides images of the original Buddha, objects associated with his life have also been revered. There is even a footprint of the Buddha, adorned with gold leaf, at a temple in Thailand.

The city of Kandy in Sri Lanka holds one of the most important relics associated with Buddhism. The sacred tooth of the Buddha is said to be preserved there, in the Temple of the Tooth. Every August it is paraded around the city on the back of an elephant in one of Asia's largest and most colourful celebrations.

The tooth relic is kept in the temple behind a gilt railing and a silver table. A gold-plated reliquary serves as the outermost of seven caskets,

SIDDHARTHA GAUTAMA

The historical Buddha, named Siddhartha Gautama, lived in the 5th and 6th centuries BC in what is now northern India. At the age of 29 he abandoned life as a prince to search for an end to human suffering. Five years of wandering and meditation led him to Benares, where Siddhartha discovered the 'Middle Way', rejecting extremes of pleasure and pain. He taught that humans suffer because we are attached to people and things in a world where nothing is permanent. The right path is to rid ourselves of desire by discipline and meditation. According to the Buddha, we are trapped in an endless cycle of rebirths, reflecting our good and evil deeds.

one within another, in which it is preserved. Each casket is made of pure gold and ornamented with precious gems. When the tooth is displayed, and this is rare, it rests in a loop of gold. At certain times visitors are allowed to enter two ante-chambers and view the outside of the reliquary. Other treasures within the splendid temple include a miniature Buddha carved from a single emerald and a sitting Buddha cut from a chunk of rock crystal.

The features on all images of the Buddha have symbolic importance. The 'urna', or bump between the eyebrows, and the elongated earlobes are signs of holiness. Sitting and reclining positions have their own specific meanings, and even hand and foot positions are symbolic: if a reclining Buddha's feet are shown in line, the god is at rest; if one foot is placed in front of the other, he is represented in death.

Chola Bronze of Shiva

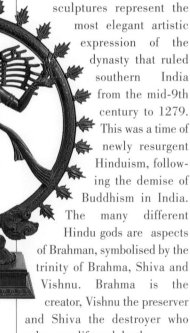

he Indian metalwork tradition dates back to small Buddhist bronzes made in the Ganges Valley in the 1st century AD. During the Gupta Dynasty, from 320 to 530, India achieved an artistic golden age, producing highly sensuous bronze sculptures. Three centuries later the Chola Dynasty revived this tradition with bronze figures in expressive dance-like poses. Lively yet serene, these sculptures represent the most elegant artistic expression of the dynasty that ruled southern India from the mid-9th century to 1279. This was a time of newly resurgent Hinduism, following the demise of Buddhism in India. The many different Hindu gods are aspects of Brahman, symbolised by the trinity of Brahma, Shiva and Vishnu. Brahma is the creator, Vishnu the preserver and Shiva the destroyer who rules over life and death.

Multi-armed gods became an accepted convention in Hindu art. The arms always appear in pairs and convey some aspect of godly power. Bronze figures of gods were produced for temple worship, and many of the best show Shiva in the form of Shiva Nataraja – a lively four-armed dancer – sometimes surrounded by a halo of fire.

Hindus believed that when Shiva danced the universe would dissolve into chaos and stars would hurtle in disorder through the skies. During a magical dance the god Shiva would first wantonly destroy the universe and then energetically re-create it. While Shiva's arms flail and his scarves fly in the wind, his facial expression shows that he is in nirvana, the state of eternal peace.

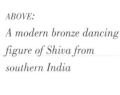

ABOVE:

A modern bronze dancing figure of Shiva from southern India

Hinduism is older than other main world religions, having its origin in the Vedism, or nature worship, that was brought to India by the Aryans in about 1500 BC. The verses which explain this, called Vedas, are still fundamental to Hindu belief. The three basic concepts in Hinduism are Samsara, Karma and Dharma. Samsara is the belief in reincarnation, that when one body dies the soul migrates to a new one. Whether this body is higher or lower in the social scale depends on Karma, action or deed. Behaviour in this life determines the status of the soul in the next. Dharma signifies faithfully following the life of the caste you are born into. Eventually, it is possible to reach nirvana, oneness with Brahma, and freedom from the perpetual cycle of death and rebirth.

This work, now in the Musée Ginet in Paris, depicts Shiva in a classic pose and reveals both the creative and destructive powers attributed to gods. His upper right and left hands hold respectively a drum which vibrates to announce creation and a flame of conflagration. His lower right hand is raised in a gesture which suggests freedom from fear, while with his lower left hand he points towards his left foot in a gesture of release. The clearest symbolism is conveyed by the action of Shiva's right foot, which boldly crushes to death the dwarf Apasmara, the demon of materialism, evil and ignorance.

Chola bronze images of the dancing figure of Shiva Nataraja symbolise both the destruction and recreation of the universe.

LEFT:
This image of Avalokitesvara in bronze and semi-precious stones is from Tibet.

CASTING

Making metal objects by open casting, mastered over 5,000 years ago, involved chiselling out of stone or baked clay and filling with molten metal, which then cooled and solidified. In the piece mould method, devised for three-dimensional items, an object was shaped in wax and covered in clay. Once dry, the clay was cut down the middle and the wax removed. The mould was then reassembled and filled with molten metal. Hollow casting involved suspending a solid object in the centre of a mould and pouring molten metal around it.

The Crown of the Holy Roman Empire

Known also as the German Imperial Crown and the Nuremburg Crown, the magnificent Crown of the Holy Roman Empire was made at Reichenau Abbey (now south-western Germany) sometime during the 10th century. It was used by many German kings when they were crowned Holy Roman Emperor by the Pope.

The crown consists of eight arched panels of gold which are hinged to form a circlet. Four of these panels are entirely covered with precious and semiprecious stones – amethysts, sapphires, emeralds and pearls. The stones are set in high relief and elaborated with filigree. The other four panels contain champlevé enamelling (see panel) depicting religious scenes. These are framed with jewels set in a filigree border.

The Imperial Crown was originally housed in Nuremburg but was hidden in Vienna as Napoleon marched towards the city. Napoleon desperately wanted the crown for his own coronation in 1804, but he never found its secret location. In 1938 Hitler insisted that the crown be returned to Nuremburg and it was buried in a salt mine during the war. Allied troops discovered the treasure, however, and the crown was restored to its place in Vienna, where it is now displayed with a fine collection of other jewels in the Schatzkammer Kunsthistorisches Museum in the old Hapsburg Palace. Another crown, also in Vienna, was made for the emperor in 1602 and fashioned like a helmet. Another treasure from the 9th century, known to have belonged to Charlemagne when he was Emperor of Europe, is a gold pendant set, on the back, with a huge cabochon sapphire in a filigree border set with garnets, emeralds and pearls. (Originally there were cabochon sapphires on both sides of the pendant but the front one,

RIGHT:

The magnificent Talisman of Charlemagne from the end of the 11th century, at Conques Abbey in France.

---

now missing, has been replaced by an oval cabochon of blue glass.) The most notable feature of this object is that between the two large cabochons are relics of what is said to be the Virgin's hair and a fragment of the True Cross.

Charlemagne, who had become king of the Franks in 768, had supported the Pope in his efforts to rid Italy of barbarian Lombard invaders and, in December 800, Pope Leo III called him to Rome and crowned him the first Holy Roman Emperor. Charlemagne's crowning had a major effect on the artistry of western Europe. He decreed that jewels should be reserved for the nobility and royalty, and the treasures that survive from the 9th and 10th centuries are generally those preserved in cathedrals and other religious sites.

It is ironic that this pendant was buried with Charlemagne when he died in 814, as he had decreed that burying jewels with the dead should cease. When the tomb was opened in about the year 1000, Otto III recovered the jewel which had been placed on Charlemagne's neck as a protective talisman. It was preserved as a cathedral treasure until 1804 and then given to the Empress Josephine to wear at her coronation. In 1914 it was donated to Reims Cathedral and is now displayed at the Palais du Tau, Reims.

The 10th-century German Imperial Crown used by Holy Roman Emperors is known by a variety of names, including the 'Crown of Charlemagne' – though no evidence suggests that it was used by him.

CHAMPLEVÉ

A variation on cloisonné enamelling, champlevé, (literally meaning 'raised field') – as used on the German Imperial Crown – is a technique in which the cells to be filled with enamel are made by gouging cavities out of a metal base, rather than building a framework of cells attached to the base. Thicker metal is needed for this method than for cloisonné and the cavities were sometimes made by acid etching rather than chiselling. Base metals such as copper or bronze were frequently used in champlevé work.

The development of transparent enamels led to a more refined form of champlevé called 'basse-taillé' in which a graded colour effect is achieved by varying the depth of incision in the surface of the metal. This technique began in Italy in the 13th century and gradually spread to other countries in western Europe.

The Golden Altarpiece of St Mark's

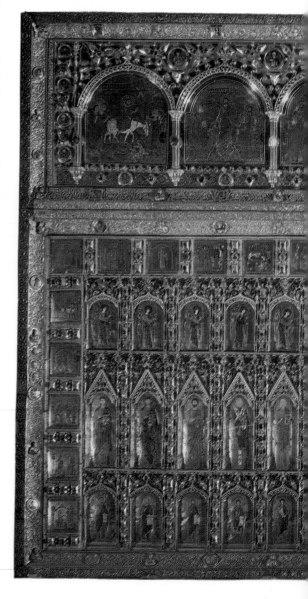

Many treasures have accumulated in the unique city of Venice and a large number of these are now housed in the treasury of St Mark's. The first Basilica di San Marco was consecrated in 832 but this burned down and the foundations of the present building were laid in the 11th century. Most of the magnificent church we see today was complete by the early 16th century.

In the late 1700s Napoleon's systematic looting of Italian treasures became legendary. His conquests were followed by treaties that required the handing over of many precious works of art. Italians were made honorary Frenchmen, and the wholesale removal of treasures from Italy was described as simply gathering the heritage of France. A considerable quantity of gemstones was filched from Venice at that time, and items taken from St Mark's alone were melted down into over 55 bars of silver and gold.

While Napoleon captured the bronze horses of St Mark's and took them to Paris, he missed a much more glittering prize. French soldiers left the remarkable Pala d'Oro (Golden Altarpiece) in St Mark's, having been told that it was worthless. The legendary tale is that a sacristan waved his arms contemptuously at the altar, saying it was all merely 'glass'. It seems likely that this was an

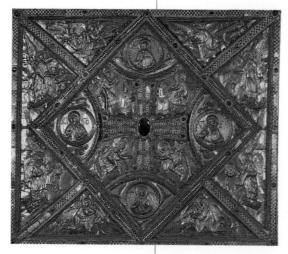

ABOVE:

The magnificent 9th-century silver and gold altar in the church of Sant' Ambrogio in Milan is another of Italy's great masterpieces of metalworking.

ingenious ruse, as a 1796 inventory of the altarpiece and a painstaking count of the gems that decorated it had revealed a very different story: in addition to cloisonné enamelling on gold, there were 1,300 pearls, 400 garnets, 300 sapphires, 300 emeralds, 90 amethysts, 75 pink and rose spinels, 50 rubies, 4 topazes and 2 cameos, making a glittering total of 2,521 precious and semiprecious stones.

The Pala d'Oro was created in four phases over the course of nearly 500 years, the earliest work consisting of medallions made by Byzantine goldsmiths in the 10th century. The enamels framing three sides of the altarpiece are 12th-century Venetian craftwork, depicting scenes from the New Testament and the life of St Mark, while those around the centrepiece date from 1209 and were brought as trophies to Venice from Constantinople. The last craftsman to work on the

Pala d'Oro was a Venetian goldsmith, Gianpaolo Buoninsegna, who gave it its present form in 1345 when he added a splendid series of plaques depicting Christ enthroned, surrounded by the Evangelists, prophets, apostles and angels.

While much has been lost, the treasury of St Mark's still contains about 300 pieces including beautiful icons, reliquaries and vessels in precious stones. The sack of Constantine in 1204 brought it many new treasures such as an elegant goblet with base, handles and lid in gold filigree ornamented with precious stones.

Another magnificent Italian church treasure is the sumptuous high altar made in about 835 for the church of Sant' Ambrogio, Milan. Wrought in silver and gold and ornamented with filigree, enamels and exquisite narrative relief scenes, it is signed by Wolvinus Magister, who received training in the courts of Charlemagne.

AMETHYSTS

Amethysts are a variety of transparent quartz, usually deep purple to pale bluish-violet in colour. In Greek the word amethyst means 'not drunken', and wearing the stone was meant to guard against intoxication. Many Romans had rings made from amethysts to help them survive the endless round of festivities. The amethyst has also been credited with the power to promote love and to repel locusts from crops. It was also claimed that amethysts would preserve their owners from blindness, strangulation or choking, and that they would improve the complexion and prevent hair falling out. Perhaps the strangest claim of all was that they offered protection against deceit and imprisonment.

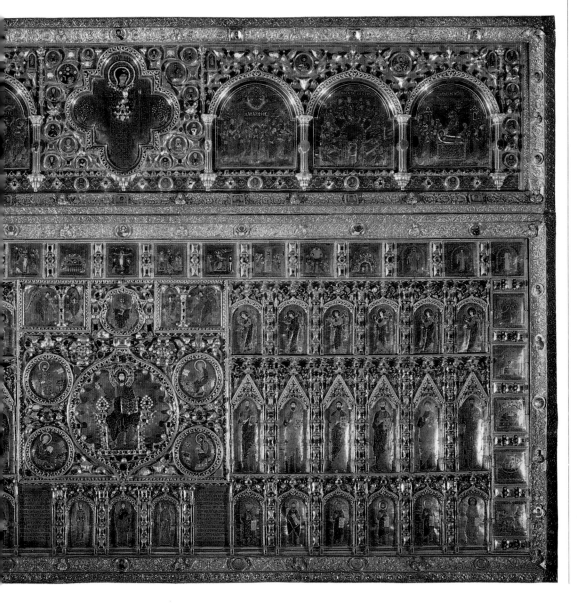

LEFT:
The Pala d'Oro measures a mere 11½ ft by 5 ft (3m by 1m) and is ornamented with thousands of fine stones, pearls and enamelled religious scenes.

Caja de las Agatas

At Oviedo cathedral, in north-western Spain, is a splendid gold reliquary ornamented with agate inlay and red enamel bands worked in gold. On its base are the symbols of the four evangelists. The top of the lid is a truncated pyramid with sloping sides richly decorated with precious stones cut en cabochon (see panel opposite).

Oviedo developed from a settlement around a Benedictine monastery founded in 761 in the fertile plains of Asturia. The Moors destroyed the town in 789 but Alfonso II rebuilt it. As king in the 9th century, Alfonso

RIGHT:

Designs on the Caja de las Agatas reliquary include birds face to face on either side of a tree. Other areas of ornament depict highly stylised birds sitting beside each other.

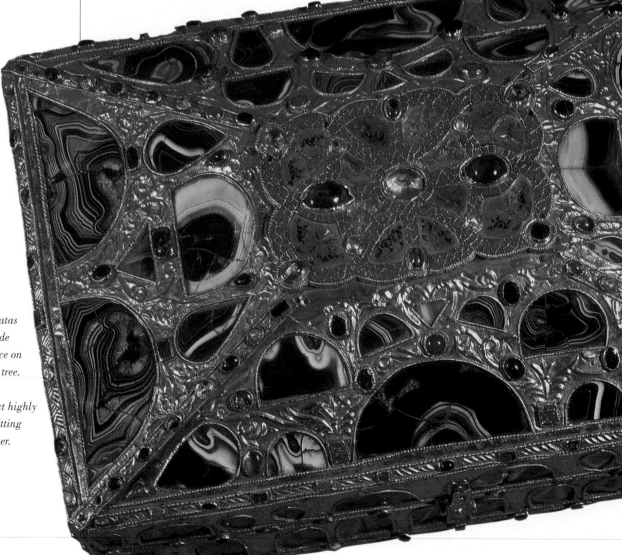

built a chapel called the Cámara Santa, now the inner sanctuary of Oviedo Cathedral, to house holy relics. These include a gem-encrusted and much treasured Cruz de los Angeles (Angel's Cross), dating from about 808, two Byzantine ivory diptychs from the 6th and 14th centuries and a highly ornamented Cruz de la Victoria, given to the church in 908. The most spectacular of them all, however, is the Caja de las Agatas, presented to the cathedral in 910 by Fuela II, who then ruled Asturia.

The Visigoths had been the masters of the Iberian peninsula from 469, and at its greatest extent their kingdom had included not only all of Spain but also Gaul as far north as the Loire River. The mountains of northern Spain formed a retreat for nobles when the Iberian kingdom was overrun by Muslim invaders and collapsed in 711.

Excavation of 6th- and 7th-century Visigothic burial sites has revealed a wonderful diversity of treasures, including belt clasps decorated with red almandine stones. Some of the brooches and buckles are fashioned from bronze, others from silver. One of the finest hoards of metalwork was found in the 19th century in an area near Toledo, which had been the Visigoths' capital. Called the Guarrazar Treasure, this collection originally included 11 weighty gold crowns decorated with repoussé, *opus interrasile* and chasing. These were broken up and sold in pieces but a goldsmith reconstructed nine of them, smuggled them to France and sold them to the government. The crowns were housed in the Cluny Museum in Paris until the 1940s when six were brought back to the Museo Arqueologica in Madrid. Some are encrusted with precious or semiprecious stones and ornamented with

pendants inscribed with letters cut out of sheet gold.

Two of the crowns in the Guarrazar Treasure have been identified as belonging to Swinthila and Recceswinth, Visigothic kings of the mid-7th century. Swinthila was the first Visigothic king to rule all of Spain and Recceswinth is most remembered for his code of laws. As the crowns are suspended from chains, they may have been votive crowns given to a church in fulfilment of a religious vow. The Visigoths had adopted orthodox Catholicism late in the 6th century. Although the influence of Germanic metalworking techniques was often evident in Visigothic art, items in the Guarrazar treasure depict plant and animal motifs from the Mediterranean and the East.

EN CABOCHON

Gemstones cut en cabochon, as on the Caja de las Agatas, may be rectangular, oval, round, square or even octagonal in shape but all are cut in such a way that the upper surface is domed. This style of cutting was used in ancient times and it continued to be widespread until the 15th century when techniques of faceting (cutting in flat planes) were developed. Facets may be cut so that light entering from above is reflected back through the top of the stone, showing its refractive properties to best advantage. Besides the simple cabochons, with domes of varying steepness, there is also a 'hollow cabochon' in which the interior of a stone is cut away to make a shell-like form.

Three Kings' Reliquary

RELIQUARIES

Receptacles known as reliquaries were generally made to preserve the remains of a sacred person – the blood, teeth or bones of a martyr, for example – or an artefact connected with some sacred event, such as a piece of the True Cross. They usually took the form of richly decorated rectangular caskets, or sometimes purse-shaped gold containers richly studded with jewels. When the relic to be preserved was a fragment of a martyr's or saint's body, the container was often made in human form. The reliquary of Ste Foy is an example of this, but is one of the very few representing an entire figure.

The Shrine, or Reliquary, of the Three Kings is one of the most magnificent examples of a religious casket of its kind. Part of the treasury of Cologne Cathedral in Germany, this is probably the most important of the reliquaries housed there.

It is one of the masterpieces of the great enamellist and goldsmith Nicholas of Verdun (*fl. c*1150–1210). Considered at the time to be the finest exponent of his art, Nicholas was an itinerant craftsman who would travel to the site of each commission. His best known work is perhaps the altarpiece of the Abbey Church of Klosterneuburg, near Vienna in Austria. The scenes depicted on this altarpiece, including Moses on Mt Sinai, were the most ambitious of their kind at the time, and this piece is considered to be among the most important surviving examples of medieval enamel work.

Although much of the work on the Three Kings' Reliquary was carried out by his assistants, the general design and figures of the prophets are by Nicholas and have been called the most important metal sculptures of the period.

Other highly significant examples are the reliquary of SS Piatus and Nicasius in Belgium's Tournai Cathedral and

the shrines of St Anne in Sieburg and of St Albanus in St Pantaleon, Cologne, although these have suffered greatly from restoration.

Of similar importance to Christian art, but from an earlier period, is a small statue made in about 980. The isolated church of Ste Foy at Conques, on the rugged slopes of a sparsely populated valley in south-west France, was built in the 11th century to house the reliquary statue and other relics of Ste Foy, a virgin martyr. The skull and girdle of Ste Foy are held preserved inside the hollow statuette. She is shown seated on a throne decorated with jewels and rock-crystal spheres, wearing a gem-encrusted robe and a heavy crown. Many of the jewels and cameos were votive offerings from believers who came to visit the relic. This was one of the pilgrimage churches on the way to Santiago de Compostela in Spain.

German goldsmiths of the 11th and 12th centuries produced a range of jewellery showing great skill and delicacy, but very little personal jewellery was made in England and France at that time. One reason for this was the fashion for a style of tunic which left little scope for jewels, with the exception of belt buckles. One important contemporary example is an ornamented gilt bronze buckle made by Nicholas of Verdun, with fine, realistically modelled figures showing characteristics similar to his other work.

ABOVE:
The bronze gilt Barbarossa 'head' reliquary of about 1160 is just over 12in (31.4cm) high.

LEFT:
The magnificent Shrine of the Three Kings reliquary casket, designed by Nicholas of Verdun, dates from the 2nd half of the 12th century.

BELOW:
Devoted followers came to pay homage to the 10th-century image of Ste Foy. The seated figure, with arms outstretched and a fixed gaze, is less than 37in (94cm) high, but is studded with an impressive array of precious stones.

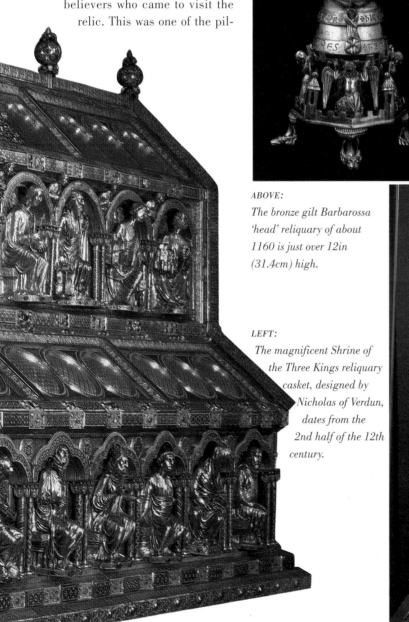

The Crown of St Stephen

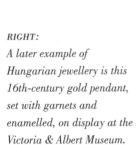

Hungary's Crown of St Stephen, which is now displayed at the country's National Museum in Budapest, has great legendary importance: Stephen (*c*975–1038), the first Christian king of Hungary, was sent the crown by Pope Sylvester II, who was regarded as having magical powers. When Stephen was canonized in 1083 the headpiece assumed a special significance.

The two main sections of the crown were made at different times and then assembled in about 1108–16. The lower section consists of a gold forehead band edged with pearls and set with cloisonné-enamelled blue and green triangular and semicircular plates. These are decorated with large gemstones and Byzantine enamelled miniatures portraying saints. The upper section has carved plates joined to form arches, decorated with enamelled plaques and gemstones. Gold chains are suspended from each side, holding ornaments set with rubies. A cross sits on top of the crown.

The colourful history of the crown has involved many changes of ownership. In 1301 King Wenceslas carried it off with him to Bohemia and then handed it over to Otto, reigning prince of Bavaria. Otto apparently lost it in a marsh. Though badly bent, it was eventually recovered and, in 1439, the widow of King Albert passed it to the Emperor Frederick IV, who kept it at his court in Vienna. When Joseph II acceded to the Hungarian throne in 1780 he had the crown placed in the imperial treasury.

During the 1848 War of Independence it was buried in what is now Romania and was then taken once more to Vienna. The last constitutional use of the crown was in 1916, when it was used for the coronation of Charles I, Emperor of Austria. A special room was then set aside for it in the palace at Buda with a crown guard of 24 men. Here it stayed until 1944. As the Red Army approached Budapest, a train was loaded with Hungarian valuables – documents, gold and jewels – to be transferred to the United States for safekeeping. With this hoard was a massive black trunk, securely locked and heavily guarded, containing

RETURNING THE TREASURE

Treasures that are bought, looted or transferred for safekeeping from their place of origin have often been the subject of emotional dispute between countries. In the early 1950s the United States resisted demands from the Hungarian government for the return of St Stephen's Crown, but by the mid-1970s America was becoming more sympathetic to Hungarian entreaties and in 1977 finally agreed to its restitution. When the crown made its way home in early 1978, the American government emphasised that they were returning the crown to the Hungarian people, and it was accepted by Hungary simply as a museum treasure which no longer had any constitutional significance.

the Crown of St Stephen. It was 34 years before this ancient relic was returned by the Americans to its home in Budapest.

Ironically, experts who examined the crown in 1981 suggested it might not be the one that Pope Sylvester II sent to Stephen. According to some, that original crown was probably returned to Rome shortly after Stephen's death and its whereabouts are now a mystery. Whatever the full story, the splendid crown now on display in Budapest is undoubtedly Hungarian and of great antiquity.

St Stephen's Crown is only one of many fine metallic and jewelled treasures with Hungarian associations. Gold was plentiful in Hungary and the art of the goldsmith flourished there in the Middle Ages. A distinctive item of Hungarian jewellery which appeared in the 18th and 19th centuries was the 'pretzel' bracelet, which used a twisted pretzel, sometimes ornamented with a floral design in gemstones, as its central motif.

Empress Gisela's Brooch

OPPOSITE:

*The famous Gisela Brooch
has an eagle, a symbol of
majestic power, as its central
motif.*

RIGHT :

*The 12th-century Eltenberg
Reliquary has four ivory
plaques depicting the
Nativity, the Three Magi, the
Crucifixion and the Holy
Women at the Sepulchre.*

In 1880 a collection of jewellery was found in a cellar in Mainz, Germany. It consisted of items believed to have been worn by the Empress Gisela at her wedding in Rome to Conrad II, German king and Holy Roman Emperor, in 1027. More recent opinion suggests the jewellery may have been made about a century later, but it is nonetheless known as the Treasure of Empress Gisela. The hoard includes necklaces, rings and brooches decorated with gemstones and other articles ornamented with filigree work and cloisonné enamelling.

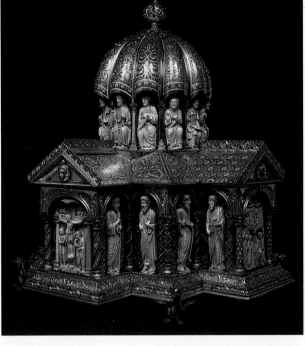

Four of the items are now in Mittelrheinisches Landesmuseum, Mainz, among them the famous Gisela Brooch, a large, circular gold brooch displaying a heraldic eagle with spread wings and outturned claws. The bird's head, tail and wings have cloisonné enamel decoration in dark blue, turquoise, green and white. The enamel which once adorned its breast is now missing and only the outline of the feathers, as marked by the cloisons, remains to indicate where it was. Above the eagle's head is a group of three sapphires. The openwork border in a raised filigree design is decorated with floral motifs of translucent green enamel.

Jewellery using animal and bird images, described as 'zoomorphic', has been produced for thousands of years in a variety of cultures. The eagle has often been associated with the gods of power and war, and, on the Gisela Brooch, is probably meant to signify imperial power. It was believed that the eagle could fly higher than any other bird, hence its symbolism of majesty.

Brooches of the 11th century were generally round, foreshadowing in design the ring-brooch which had become the most popular form of jewellery by the 13th century; it was frequently given as a love token or as a gift between friends.

Another important medieval treasure is the Eltenberg Reliquary fashioned in Cologne in about 1180. Made of copper and bronze gilt with ivory figures, it is a fine example of champlevé enamelling (see page 59).

Around the dome are seated Christ and 11 of his apostles, with 16 figures of prophets holding inscribed scrolls (the first two are 19th-century replacements). At the time of the French Revolution the reliquary was kept in a Benedictine nunnery at Eltenberg on the German/Dutch border. In the early 19th century it was hidden in a chimney, and it then passed through several owners before arriving at its present home in London's Victoria and Albert Museum. The main centres of this art were Cologne (see pages 64–5), Trier and Aachen; other significant 12th-century works include a fine altar by goldsmith Eibert at Welfenschatz.

SAPPHIRES

Sapphires are a variety of transparent corundum, a hexagonal crystal found in any colour except red (red corundums being rubies) though the most usual colour is blue. The best quality blue stones come from Kashmir, and others from Myanmar (Burma) and Sri Lanka, where the skilful faceting of sapphires has become an important industry. Star sapphires (which reflect light in a star shape when cut en cabochon) are regarded as tokens of good luck. Like other gems, sapphires were pulverised and taken medicinally: a 1628 treatise claimed they not only cured melancholy but would also help dysentery, heart disease, skin ailments and inflammation. An emblem of chastity, the sapphire was often set in rings worn by the clergy.

Our Lady of Vladimir Icon

RIGHT AND FAR RIGHT:
The richly jewelled icon of Our Lady of Vladimir is made of gold, enamel and niello. It is now in St Petersburg's Russia Museum.

CENTRE:
Finland's Our Lady Burial Icon (the Virgin of Kazin), decorated with pearls and gems, was made at the Old Valermo monastery in the 19th century.

Metalworking dates from the 3rd millennium BC around the area of modern-day Russia, but the beginnings of Russian art are generally associated with the introduction of Christianity in 988–9. Vladimir, The Grand Duke of Kievan Russia, chose Greek Orthodoxy as his faith – a move which led to the forging of close links with Byzantium in art as well as religion. Vladimir ordered that all connections with pagan worship should be destroyed.

'Icon' is a Greek word meaning 'image' which was used to identify the sacred religious pictures of the Greek Orthodox Church. The Russians adopted the art and developed it further, the city of Novgorod becoming an important centre of religious painting. Their earliest surviving icons date from the 12th century and are masterpieces of religious art.

Contacts between Novgorod and Constantinople led the Greek artist Theophanes – one of the greatest religious painters of the 14th century – to move to Russia. It was at about this time that the studding of icons with jewels was introduced, to be followed by the custom of casing them in elaborate metal frames that covered the painting almost entirely, leaving exposed only the faces, hands and sometimes other details, such as halos.

Early icons were generally fairly large as they were made for use in churches and for carrying in processions. Many formed part of an iconostasis, a screen with doors and several tiers of icons, which served to separate the nave from the sanctuary in the Eastern Church. Iconostases, usually with three but sometimes with as many as five tiers of icons, became a feature of Russian Orthodox churches early in the 14th century. From the 15th century onwards, a demand for smaller icons, which could be used in private chapels, steadily developed in Moscow. And, as citizens became more prosperous, it became usual to place an icon in the corner of each room of a house and at the head of each bed.

The original icon of Our Lady of Vladimir is a Byzantine work dating from about 1130. It was brought to Russia in 1131 and placed in the cathedral at Vladimir but was moved to Moscow in 1395. The painting itself is one of the finest of all surviving early icons and has been copied by many artists. The tender way in which the Virgin inclines her head towards the child has ensured the picture's lasting appeal.

Icons other than those intended for church or processional use were usually made as wall ornaments, but some very small ones were designed to be worn as pendants in triptych form. A 17th-century Russian silver triptych pendant with enamelled icon is displayed at the Victoria and Albert Museum in London.

A most unusual and important treasure of the Orthodox Church Museum of Finland in Kuopio is the Virgin of Kazin icon illustrated here. For much of its history Finland has been torn between Sweden and Russia – it only achieved independence in 1917 – but many fine objects have fortunately survived the country's struggles and upheavals and have been successfully preserved.

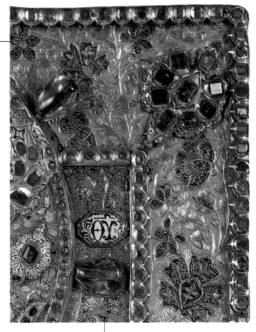

NIELLO

A black powdered compound of sulphur and silver, lead or copper known as niello can be used to decorate metal in the same way as enamel, and is usually intended to darken the indented portions of linear designs. Once the niello has been applied to a metal object, the metal is heated and the powdered alloy melts and becomes fused in the grooves and depressions. When cool, the metal is polished until the niello is removed on the raised parts. Niello decoration has been found on ancient articles such as spearheads, but the technique was probably first applied to jewellery by the Romans in about the 3rd century. It was also used by the Egyptians, early Byzantines and Anglo-Saxons.

Queen Constanza's Crown

Heavy gold mesh decorated with coloured stones makes the crown of Queen Constanza of Aragon a delicate and most unusual royal headdress. She was the wife of Emperor Frederick II, Holy Roman Emperor from 1220 to 1250. The crown, which is now in Palermo Cathedral in Sicily, has a framework of stylised floral bands decorated with seed

ABOVE:
The Iron Crown of Lombardy has a band of iron around the inside which legend says was made from a nail of the True Cross.

pearls and enamel, one encircling the base and the other two forming arches which cross at the apex. Around the gold head band are 16 *fleurs-de-lis*.

Another royal crown of exceptional beauty is to be seen at the cathedral at Monza, where it is carried in a solemn annual procession. This simple diadem has six hinged gold panels, each with an enamel background and a large central stone surrounded by rosettes beaten in repoussé. Called the Iron Crown of Lombardy, it was thought to have belonged to Theodolinda, the 7th-century queen of the Lombards, but its design and workmanship in fact suggest that it was probably fashioned about two centuries later. Whatever the crown's exact

origin, it was definitely used in coronation ceremonies of the kings of Italy throughout the Middle Ages, and in that of the Holy Roman Emperor Frederick Barbarossa. In 1530 Charles V was crowned with it in Bologna.

The cathedral treasury of Monza has other fine objects besides the crown, including a 9th-century reliquary purse said to hold the teeth of St John the Baptist. Set into its richly decorated filigree surface are 186 gemstones and 20 large pearls, while its border is decorated with 130 small pearls.

While the Iron Crown of Lombardy was probably made sometime after the 7th century, one magnificent jewelled item is definitely from the reign of Queen Theodolinda: a gospel cover dated about 603, which was given to her by Pope Gregory the Great on the occasion of the baptism of her son Archibald. Queen Theodolinda had helped convert many Lombards to Christianity and the Pope expressed his gratitude to her with this gift. Made in Rome, the gold cover is embellished with two crosses surrounded by cloisonné enamel and set with 110 gems and eight antique cameos. The gems include pearls, sapphires, amethysts, peridots (emeralds), garnets, rubies and topazes. All of the stones are finely cut and polished and are mounted in a style very characteristic of medieval lapidary work, when the preference was for simple, geometric shapes.

Towards the end of the 13th century, a French law was passed which forbade commoners to wear precious stones, pearls or circlets of silver and gold; the wearing of jewels became the exclusive privilege of the elite. The 13th and 14th centuries were times of splendid royal jewels, most of which were reserved for ceremonial occasions, and goldsmiths put their energy into creating magnificent crowns: Edward II of England reportedly owned ten crowns in 1324.

LEFT:
At each side of the 13th-century crown of Queen Constanza hang pendants of gold links decorated with enamel.

DIADEMS AND CROWNS

A diadem can be any ornamental headband, and is often worn as a symbol of sovereignty. Early variations which appeared in Greece and Rome evolved from wreaths of leaves. In the Middle Ages, Western European rulers wore a chaplet, or ornamental band, and later a band of hinged plaques with enamelled and jewelled decoration. Though Anglo-Saxon crowns were occasionally square, most are circular or semicircular. Some are used only for coronations; others for state occasions; a votive crown is used as a religious offering and a funerary crown is for burial. A coronet can be worn by someone of high rank but lower than a sovereign.

Islamic Kursi

The religion of Islam was founded in the Near East in the 7th century by the prophet Muhammad. Born in Mecca around 570, he became a merchant and, in about 610, went into the mountains to meditate. His mission was to preach a new faith centred on the one true God, Allah. He went out delivering the message but was driven out of Mecca in 622; his now famous flight to Medina is taken as the date for the start of the Muslim era.

In 630, when Muhammad returned and took control of Mecca, the city became the focus for the new religion. The Holy Book of Islam, the Koran (Quran), embodies Muhammad's teachings and sets out principles covering every aspect of life. Muslims believe it is the direct word of Allah as revealed to his prophet. It is on these writings, together with the Hadith, a collection of Muhammad's sayings, that the entire culture of Islam was based.

Many fine objects have been created for Islamic worship. The 14th-century kursi illustrated is a cabinet for holding the Koran. It is made of brass with inlaid silver and engraved designs. Ewers (with or without spouts) and accompanying basins are used in religious observance for ritual purification. They are made of beaten brass and inlaid with gold, silver and copper. Inlay involves the hammering of the decorative metal into an area that has been previously grooved or hammered out. All these religious objects reflect the high artistry of metalworking during Mamluk rule; they are now to be seen in Cairo's Museum of Islamic Art.

The Mamluks were originally the Turkish slaves of the Ayyubid rulers of Egypt (the word Mamluk means 'owned'), and the first Mamluk dynasty, the Bahri, who came to power in 1250, was descended from these slaves. The Mamluks ruled both Egypt and part of Syria until the conquest by Ottoman Turks in the early 16th century.

While Mamluk metalworking inherited the tradition of inlaid brasswork, craftsmen developed a style all their own. In many of the basins, ewers, trays, candlesticks and incense burners they produced, silver and gold inlay was often accompanied by engraved inscriptions and rich floral designs. A number of inscriptions included the name of the sultan for whom the object was made. Arabic writing became a decorative feature of Islamic art, often used on metalwork to create a complex repeating pattern.

Other important survivals from the Mamluk period include bronze-covered wooden Koran boxes inlaid with silver and gold, steel helmets decorated with gold wire and brass mosque lanterns.

The explosive spread of Islam was one of the most important movements in world history. In less than 80 years after Muhammad's death in 632, the new religion had been carried from the Arabian peninsula into Central Asia in the east and as far as the Atlantic coast of Africa and Spain in the west. Islam brought a unifying, stabilising force and political order to vast areas of the world.

BELOW:
Fine Islamic brass ewers and basins inlaid with precious metals were made in 14th-century Egypt.

OPPOSITE:
Muslims keep their holy book, the Koran, in a kursi. This 14th-century brass cabinet shows skilled use of inlay and engraving.

BRASS

Inlaid brass was a speciality of the Near East, as shown on these fine objects. Brass is an alloy of copper and zinc, using a varying proportion of each metal. The Romans first used brass for making coins and commemorative plates, and the alloy had became fairly common by the 1st century AD.

Punching and embossing techniques are often used to decorate brassware. Craftsmen use a variety of punches of different shapes and sizes, holding the vessel against a block of lead or pitch. This allows the worked brass to stretch without cracking. Because brass can be cut and filed easily, it is also suitable for openwork designs. Dutch brass tea caddies made in the 18th century are a good example of this pierced metalwork technique.

'Tombac' is a copper/zinc alloy which produces another type of brass for jewellery. When beaten into thin foil to imitate gold leaf, tombac is referred to as Dutch metal or Dutch gold.

Cameo Brooches

ABOVE:

This fine French cameo, incised on a spiral shell and framed in a 17th-century mount, is now in the Bargello Museum, Florence.

The brooch shown here is a fine example of a 'figural brooch', a type of ring brooch with a rim shaped like a floral stem. Typically, the nodes of the stem were punctuated with pearls and in the centre were figures or animals made of chased and enamelled gold, rubies and diamonds. A rather fine Spanish example features lions surrounded by gold and rubies. The hat badge opposite uses an enamelling technique called *émail en ronde bosse* (see panel) which creates a raised effect, almost as if the figures were carved as cameos. Figural jewellery of this kind was very popular in the 15th and 16th centuries.

The French gold brooch also featured here, from the Bargello Museum in Florence, dates from the same period and has a central cameo carved from a semiprecious stone. Gemstones with layers of different colours, such as sardonyx and cornelian, were used to show designs in low relief. The earliest carved two-colour stones dated from Sumerian times and were used as seals. Later, the Hellenistic Greeks and Romans produced cameos in low relief for ornamental jewellery. Several examples have been found of cameos cut with profile portraits of the Roman Emperor Augustus.

One rather unusual English piece called the Epsom Cameo (it was found at Epsom in Surrey) was carved on an irregularly shaped garnet and set in a gold mount. The pendant is late 7th-century but the cameo itself may be much older.

The art of cameo making, which was maintained at a moderate level throughout the Middle Ages, was considerably developed during the Renaissance. Gem engravers were employed by great Italian patrons like Lorenzo de' Medici, who commissioned a piece called the Noah Cameo. Oval in shape, it is carved from onyx and depicts Noah and his family with animals and birds leaving the ark. It is mounted in a gold frame, with floral motifs on the reverse. The doors of the ark bear the words 'LAVR MED', which was the mark of Lorenzo de' Medici. The cameo was listed in the 15th-century inventories of the Medici family and is now in the British Museum.

Another famous cameo, also Italian and made from onyx, has carved relief decoration on both sides of the same stone: Hercules is portrayed on one side with Omphale on the reverse. Dated about 1530, the cameo is set in a gold mount containing diamonds and rubies. It was given by the Emperor Charles V to Pope Clement VII and it too is now in the British Museum.

Portrait medallions were popular in the 16th century, worn suspended on a chain or ribbon around the neck. These often included cameos mounted in a frame with gemstones.

Cameos have been used in various items of jewellery, from brooches and pendants to finger rings. Besides gemstones, other hard materials such as rock crystal, coral and jet have been carved and mounted in similar ways. In a French technique called *cameo habillé* the image of a head was cut in the surface of the stone and adorned with a necklace, hair ornament or earrings made of small gemstones. These were particularly fashionable in the 19th century.

This term means enamelling an object in the round. Opaque enamel, usually white, was laid thickly on to a raised or modelled metal surface, then layers of coloured enamels were applied, the piece being refired after each application. Up to ten firings were needed to build up the decorative design. Also called 'encrusted enamel', this technique was developed in France and Spain during the 14th and 15th centuries, and became widespread in the 16th century. When only white enamel was used to create the rounded effect, the method was known as *émail en blanc*. The Dunstable Swan Jewel, a gold brooch representing a swan and dating from about the 11th century, is a famous example in which white enamel is used to create the swan's elaborate plumage. The jewel is now in the British Museum.

ABOVE:
An elaborate gold frame in the form of a wreath of leaves with red, green and blue enamelling surrounds this cameo, the property of the Kunsthistorisches Museum, Vienna. The jewel depicts four male heads in profile and uses émail en ronde bosse *to create a relief effect.*

RIGHT:
An enamelled gold version of Henry IV's Swan Badge (the device of the de Bohun family into which he married), which is known as the Dunstable Swan Jewel. It is a fine example of the white enamelling technique émail en blanc.

Aztec Headdress

When the Spanish explorer Hernan Cortés arrived in Mexico in 1521, he knew he had found the legendary 'land of gold'. The Aztecs, or Tenochcas as they called themselves, entered Mexico in about the 12th century and built a powerful empire over most of present-day Mexico. By 1350 they had founded the capital, Tenochtitlan, which grew to become Mexico City.

Aztec Indian gold-smiths were highly skilled and the Spanish expressed great admiration for the many jewels that they produced and wore. Both men and women adorned themselves with earrings, necklaces and bracelets and, in addition, men pierced both their nasal septum and their chin, enabling them to wear ornaments of crystal, shell, amber, turquoise or gold.

The Aztec leaders wore splendid feather creations on their heads, often sprinkled with pearls and precious stones. The one shown here, made from green quetzal feathers woven and studded with gold, was

RIGHT:

This splendid 16th-century feather headdress studded with gold may have been presented to Hernan Cortés by the Aztec leader Motecuhzoma the Younger.

BELOW:

A two-headed Aztec serpent mosaic, also displayed in the British Museum, which was made from turquoise as an offering to the god of healing.

reputed to be the headdress presented to Cortés by the Aztec leader Motecuhzoma the Younger. It is now in the Museum für Volkerkunde in Vienna. This is one of the few true Aztec items to survive, as most items of gold and silver that were shipped back to Spain were melted for re-use.

Another rare survival is a black mask representing Tezcatlipoca, made from a human skull with turquoise and obsidian mosaic. Tezcatlipoca was the ferocious god of war and sorcery. While the Aztecs were highly skilled in crafts, they were also fierce warriors with savage religious practices involving the regular supply of sacrificial victims to please the gods. Perhaps the most famous form of human sacrifice was that of a handsome young captive who was chosen annually to impersonate the fearsome god Tezcatlipoca. For one year he lived an honoured life with four beautiful girls as his mistresses. However, the year of pleasure had its price. At the end, he was obliged to mount the steps of the temple and lie on his back so that a flint dagger could be plunged into his chest.

A Spanish force of about 400 men managed to conquer the Aztec Empire of about 11 million people, and the weak young Aztec leader was killed. He had regarded Cortés as part of a myth of the 'returning god ruler'. Aztec resistance was further lowered by deadly epidemics of diseases such as smallpox and malaria.

The early Mexican jewellery that survives is mainly Mixtec, a culture that preceded the Aztecs and was absorbed by them. Monte Alban, a major ceremonial centre in Axcaca, was used as a Mixtec burial ground and has produced a wealth of ornaments, richly carved animal bones and lapidary work, as well as thousands of pearls, metal objects and turquoise mosaics.

OBSIDIAN

One of the semiprecious stones used in the mask of Tezcatlipoca is obsidian, solidified volcanic lava in the form of natural glass. Though it is usually black and opaque, some types are coloured and transparent.

Obsidian is especially common in objects from Pre-Columbian Mexico and antiquities found around the Mediterranean. As the stone breaks with a sharp cutting edge, Aztec and Maya Indians used it for arrowheads, knives and weapons as well as for decorative inlay.

From the time that the surface of obsidian is cut, it is exposed to air and absorbs water from the atmosphere at a constant rate. By analysing the water content of an obsidian stone, archaeologists are able accurately to determine when an object was carved.

Incan Silver Llama

The Inca Empire, covering what is now Peru, Ecuador, Bolivia and northern Chile, arose in the 1300s to become one of the world's great civilisations. Although not strictly 'sacred', all llamas,

RIGHT AND BELOW:
Chimú craftsmen used gold, sometimes ornamented with polychrome decoration, for their funerary masks. These date from the 13th century.

vicunas and alpacas were the property of the Inca emperor, along with the immensely valuable wool the animals supplied. The splendid 15th-century silver llama illustrated here, which is now displayed at the American Museum of Natural

History in New York, is typical of the plant and animal images that were placed in the gardens of Inca temples.

Large quantities of gold and silver were mined by the Incas, but they mainly used these precious metals for decoration rather than currency. To the Incas, gold contained the power of the sun. Their emperors were regarded as descendants of the sun god and were worshipped as divine beings. According to the Incan version of creation, three eggs fell from heaven, one was gold, one silver and one copper. From these eggs came the nobles, the princesses and the common people.

When the Spanish explorer Pizarro and his mercenaries defeated the Incan army in 1532, they entered the capital, Cuzco, and found great wealth in the palaces. The walls were described as 'lined with gold plates', with niches holding gold and silver animal and human figures. Even more remarkable was the Temple of the Sun, all four walls of which were reputedly covered from roof to floor with plates of gold. At harvest time, temple terraces were carpeted with artificial cornfields made completely of gold.

A vast number of Incan gold artefacts were sent back to Spain to be melted down. What survives today is mainly the treasure that was buried with the dead, as the Catholic Church disapproved of plundering burial grounds. Fortunately, bodies were buried with considerable treasure as the Incas believed the dead must pay to assure their passage into the afterlife. As with other resources, metals were controlled by the state and jewellery was made solely for the royal court.

Hoards discovered in the 20th century have revealed metallic treasures from earlier cultures assimilated by the Incas. The Mochicas, who inhabited coastal Peru in AD 100–800, were probably the earliest

metalworkers in the Andes. Among the priceless artefacts recovered from Mochica tombs are a ceremonial clock made from over 1,600 decorated gold discs, and gloves made of sheet gold, which were placed on the hands of noble dead. Another early Peruvian group, the Nasca, who lived in the 7th to 9th centuries, also produced intricate goldwork.

The most exciting archaeological discoveries were made in the 1930s in northern Peru, which was the territory of the Chimú people from about 1000 until 1470, when they were conquered by the Incas. Tens of thousands of objects were recovered, making this the greatest find of gold artefacts of any ancient civilisation. Chimú craftsmen developed techniques for welding different hues of gold into one single item. Decorations used on each object were unique, as the Chimú believed that repeating a design would offend the sensibilities of the gods. The mask shown on the facing page is now housed at the Miguel Mujica Gallo Collection in Lima.

BELOW:
An intricately crafted Columbian gold raft 8in (20.5cm) long. The standing figures wear elaborate ornamental headdresses.

LEFT:
Silver llamas were used during Incan ceremonies to encourage the fertility of these precious animals.

EMERALDS

Emeralds, a variety of beryl, are one of the most valuable and rarest of precious stones. Their green colour, which can vary from pale to quite dark green, comes from traces of chromium in the stone. Pre-Columbian Indians in South America used emeralds freely, as on the Chimú mask, often drilling them to make beads or notching them as pendants. Some Indian emeralds are exceptionally large: one, owned by Mogul rulers in Delhi, weighs 78 carats; it has an inscription in Persian around the edge reading 'He who possesses this charm shall enjoy the special protection of god'. The Maharajah of Punjab possessed a remarkable string of prayer beads made of 70 emerald stones. Besides being attractive, emeralds were thought to assist health and wellbeing. A medieval treatise advised that emeralds worn from the neck would ward off malarial chill, improve eyesight, prevent epileptic seizures and cure 'moods of fury'.

Quimbaya Popora

ndean Indians of South America wore small decorative bottles called 'poporas' (or lime flasks) around their necks as ornaments and as a convenient means of carrying lime. The practice of chewing coca leaves to fight hunger, cold and fatigue has been widespread in that area for centuries, and it was the custom to use lime to mix with the leaves.

The seated-figure popora illustrated here is made of tumbaga (see panel) and is part of a remarkable collection known as the Quimbaya Treasure. This hoard of 121

CENTRE, INSET:

A gold figure pendant representing a deity, now in the National Museum of the American Indian (Heye Foundation), New York.

RIGHT:

This pre-Columbian nose ornament is made of sheet gold with animal motifs beaten in repoussé. It is one of the items in the collection of Bogota's Museo del Oro.

items of jewellery and other articles dates from about AD 400 to 1000 and was found in the Quimbaya area of Colombia in 1891. The collection was presented to the Queen of Spain and is now housed in the Museo de America in Madrid.

Many gold objects (with a total weight of about 30 tonnes) were collected by the Spanish in South and Central America and sent back to Spain in the 16th century. Nearly all of these items were melted down for re-use, but some objects have survived. Over 5,000

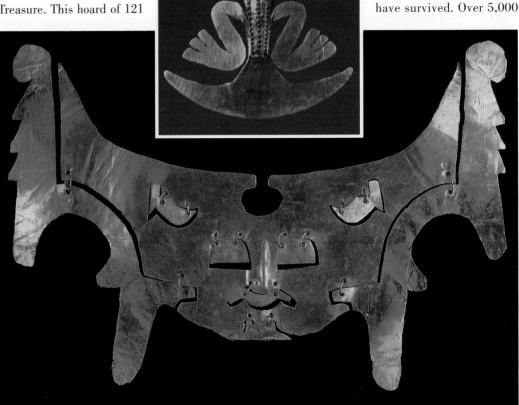

pieces of pre-Columbian jewellery made between 300 BC and the 16th century AD can now be seen in the Museo del Oro, Bogota.

It is believed that much treasure still remains in the depths of Lake Guatavita, the circular mountain lake near Bogota. When a new chief was installed, Indians threw gold offerings and emeralds into the lake from a raft to please the gods. The chief was known as El Dorado (Spanish for 'The Golden One') because he was traditionally covered in gold dust for the ceremony. One of the treasures of the Museo del Oro is a tiny pre-Columbian gold raft carved with figures acting out this important ceremony. Such scenes were depicted in small gold objects called 'tunjos', which served as votive offerings to the gods.

Another significant pre-Columbian hoard, known as the Venado Beach Treasure, which included jewellery, was discovered in the late 1940s in a cemetery near the Canal Zone of Panama. The site was excavated more fully by a team from Harvard University's Peabody Museum in 1951, when a spectacular collection of gold breastplates, bracelets, nose ornaments, pendants and three-dimensional effigy figures was recovered. Coclé jewellery, which originated from a province in Panama and was set with emeralds and other gemstones, was similar in style to the Quimbaya Treasure.

Other important hoards of pre-Columbian jewellery include the Sigsig Treasure, which was found in 1889 in southern Ecuador. Tomb items included a crown with upright plumes made of flat gold sheet, bracelets, dress ornaments and seals. Most of these are now housed in the Museum of the American Indian in New York.

BELOW:
A Colombian popora in the shape of a seated male figure from the Quimbaya Treasure. The cover would have held a spatula for extracting lime from the flask.

TUMBAGA

The lime flask shown here, and a number of other items in the Quimbaya Treasure, were made from tumbaga, which is an alloy of gold and copper (some silver also occurs naturally in the gold). Many articles of Pre-Columbian jewellery made by Indians of the Andes, Central America and Mexico contained this alloy. It has a lower melting point than copper or gold and is harder than either used in a pure form.

Tumbaga is naturally dull in colour, but could be brightened in certain areas to create a design. This process, called 'depletion gilding', used a pickle solution to dissolve the copper oxide wherever highlighting was desired, leaving a thin layer of gold on the surface; no gold was added, so this was quite different from ordinary gilding. The Indians also used a similar process, 'depletion silvering', to enhance items made of an alloy of silver and copper.

Benin Leopards

The kingdom of Benin became a powerful West African state in about 1400. Its wealth came from trade in ivory, pepper, palm oil and the notorious sale of slaves. In 1485, about 100 years after bronze casting was introduced to the country, the Portuguese began trading with Benin. In exchange for pepper, ivory and slaves, the Portuguese supplied bronze in the form of bracelets. Benin bronze casting flourished in the 16th and 17th centuries, after the imported raw material became plentiful.

Benin became a province of Nigeria in 1914 after a classic story of misunderstanding between different cultures. In 1897, a British vice-consul announced his plans to visit the *oba*, ruler of Benin. The *oba* explained that he could not receive the vice-consul that day as he would be engaged in an important local ceremony. However, the British official insisted on making the journey. Many of his party were killed en route, and, although the *oba* was not responsible for this, a punitive expedition was sent by the British the following year to plunder the royal palace and send the *oba* into exile.

The pillaging of the *oba*'s palace produced spoils consisting of over 2,000 artefacts. These included bronzes, ivories and woodcarvings: nearly a thousand heavy rectangular bronze relief plaques portraying a variety of palace characters and even Portuguese soldiers; large bronze snakes, cast in sections and attached to the roofs of the palace towers, possibly symbolic of the power of the *oba*; bronze and ivory heads of deceased royalty used in the ancestor worship that was important to Benin and much of Africa (both bronze and ivory casting were controlled by the royal court, with artisans organised into guilds). These were sent back to England and caused a sensation. The rich cultural traditions of Black Africa came to be appreciated as never before, and two books about Benin art were published in the next few years. In 1919 the Director of the Museum für Volkerkunde in Berlin praised the Benin bronzes with these words: 'Benvenuto Cellini could not have cast them better, and nobody else could either'. Some of the objects were placed in the British Museum; others were sold and are now in museums as far afield as Berlin, Vienna, St Petersburg and Dresden, as well as in private collections worldwide. Little of the Benin treasure has stayed in Nigeria for future generations of Africans to appreciate.

BELOW:

Leopards were used in Benin art to represent power. This majestic pair were carved from ivory and have copper spots.

BELOW:
When the British military expedition conquered Benin in 1898, they found this bronze queen's head, which was made in about 1500. It had been placed on an altar dedicated to the mother of King Besignie.

ABOVE:
This Benin ornamental ivory mask is surmounted by representations of the heads of Portuguese merchants.

The largest known pieces of carved ivory are African, from Zaire and the Benin area of Nigeria. While initially white, ivory becomes yellower and browner with age. It has been used in carving since ancient times in China and Japan. In Russia the tradition of ivory carving, mainly using walrus tusks, originated in the 10th century and ivory has been used more generally in Europe since the 13th century. The Erbach School was established in late 19th-century Germany for the making of ivory jewels, and artists of the Art Nouveau movement designed elegant figures as well as jewellery in which ivory was set off by bronze. While concern for endangered elephants has put restraints on the ivory trade, especially in Europe, demand for the substance remains and artisans in South and East Asia still use it.

Cellini Salt-cellar

RIGHT:

The large figures on the
Cellini salt-cellar are of the
god of the sea, Neptune, and
the goddess of the earth,
Ceres. Smaller figures
represent Night, Day,
Twilight, Dawn and the
Four Winds.

The Florentine sculptor and goldsmith Benvenuto Cellini worked under the patronage of Pope Clement VII in Rome until 1540. He then went to France to work for Francis I for five years before returning to Italy and the court of Cosimo de' Medici. Cellini has been credited with some of the finest of all Renaissance jewellery though few items can be identified as definitely his work.

One remarkable object undoubtedly made by Cellini was the great salt-cellar crafted in gold in the mid-1500s for King Francis I of France, who had given Cellini 1,000 gold crowns to be melted down for the purpose. In his memoirs of 1558 Benvenuto Cellini said the king 'exclaimed in

RIGHT:

The large figures on the Cellini salt-cellar are of the god of the sea, Neptune, and the goddess of the earth, Ceres. Smaller figures represent Night, Day, Twilight, Dawn and the Four Winds.

ABOVE:

The Belli casket was given by Pope Clement VII to the future Henry II of France and Catherine de' Medici.

astonishment and could not stop looking at it'.

Cellini's autobiography described a number of other items that he had made, such as a ring for Pope Paul III and Pope Clement VII's cope button. The button consists of a large diamond supporting a figure of God surrounded by three cherubs. Cellini's work ranged widely and included designs for coins and medals.

His writing gives a fascinating insight into the making of jewellery at that time. It also provides glimpses of troubled Italy in the years following the Sack of Rome in 1527, when 40,000 imperial troops pillaged and burned the city because they had not been paid; even the Pope was taken prisoner from May until November. Artists were caught up in the mayhem, and Cellini was one of those imprisoned. Finally, the troops were paid and order was restored.

Another great example of Italian Renaissance work is a magnificent casket of rock crystal mounted in silver gilt and enamelled. This was fashioned by Valerio Belli over the two years 1530–2 and is now in Florence's Museo degli Argenti. The casket was just one of many fine objects commissioned by the Medici Pope Clement VII, a powerful figure in the 16th century,

Clement believed in taking large doses of powdered gems internally. Crushed-jewel remedies were very fashionable at the time and in 1534 he was given enormous quantities of powdered gems over a period of 14 days, the most expensive of which was a diamond. There was a considerable trade in providing the wealthy infirm with as much of this treatment as they could digest.

ROCK CRYSTAL

Rock crystal is a type of crystalline natural quartz, generally known simply as crystal. Usually colourless and transparent, it is harder than glass and has been used by artisans for centuries. It became popular among craftsmen in medieval Egypt, Iraq and Persia, and was particularly valued in Renaissance times. The magnificent Belli casket has carved panels which illustrate how decorative the stone can be. It is still used for bracelets, beads and earrings. Crystal can be either faceted or merely polished, though in recent times it is less likely to be faceted as lead glass is much more easily available. Rock crystal has been to the Japanese what jade has been to the Chinese – a highly prized symbol of purity. The Japanese held dragons to be the supreme creative powers of the universe, and believed small quartz crystals to be formed by the breath of the White Dragon and larger crystals by that of the Purple Dragon.

Howard Grace Cup

owards the end of the 14th century there was a revival of fine silver engraving in Europe and, for the next two hundred years, a growing fashion for mounting objects in gold and silver. Explorers and merchants brought all manner of treasures back to Europe from India, China, Africa and the West Indies in the 15th and 16th centuries. Besides shells, gourds, horns, coconuts and other natural objects, travellers also brought artefacts from closer to home, such as fine Venetian glass, Baltic amberware and Turkish coloured pottery. These objects were often set in decorative metal mounts

RIGHT:

The Studley Bowl, now in the Victoria and Albert Museum, shows the decorative use of engraved lettering and floral sprays in fine silverware of the late 14th century.

INSET BELOW:

A detail of the silver engraving on the cover of the Studley Bowl.

to make cups and beakers, or placed on more spectacular stands for display.

The Howard Grace Cup, hallmarked 1525, bears the inscriptions VINUM TUUM BIBE CUM GAUDIO and ESTOTE SOBRII on the mounts of the cup and cover. These are injunctions to temperance, similar to those found on other medieval cups. It was most probably the cup bequeathed to Catherine of Aragon in 1513 by Lord Admiral Sir Edward Howard, who commissioned the fine mountings. The figure of St George on the cover was probably added at the end of the 15th century.

By the middle of the 16th century the idea of mounting objects in metal had gained enormous popularity. The treatment was even applied to stoneware pots, and for mottled tigerware jugs from Germany it was especially favoured. Glass, which was still a rarity, was as highly valued in England as elsewhere. A mount of silver gilt made in 1546 shows off superbly a milky white Venetian glass jug which once belonged to Catherine Parr, sixth wife of Henry VIII.

Another fine mounted object is the Wan-Li Ewer, dating from the 16th or early 17th centuries, which combined Chinese Ming porcelain with English silver-gilt mounts. After the 1520s finely decorated objects in Ming porcelain began to be brought to England, where they were often mounted in silver, gold or silver-gilt and used as a fashionable and luxurious accompaniment to a banqueting service.

A ewer and basin were seen as essential elements on dining tables throughout the Middle Ages and for some time later. Until forks came into common use it was necessary for diners to wash their hands before and after a meal. A treatise of 1480 recommended allowing those more worthy to wash first, and refraining from spitting in the basin after washing. Those who could not afford silver ewers and basins used baser metals, such as copper and brass. By the mid-18th century, however, ewers and basins had become mere sideboard ornaments and few were made after the end of the century.

LEFT:
The Howard Grace
Cup has an ivory
font-shaped cup and a
cover and mount in
silver-gilt set with
pearls and garnets.

THE ROGERS SALT

Of all the precious mounted objects, those made of rock crystal are among the most splendid ever produced. Queen Elizabeth I possessed over 50 cups, bowls and ewers of crystal, and many of these were set handsomely in gold or silver-gilt.

The great state salt-cellars produced during her reign, such as the Rogers Salt dating from about 1601, were usually mounted. This was one of the last great Tudor mounted salt-cellars ever made, and has a cylinder of crystal with a parchment roll painted with flowers and the arms of the Goldsmiths' Company. The goldsmiths, who included workers in both silver and gold, received their Royal Charter in 1327.

While some important mounted pieces have survived, many mounts were being melted down by the year 1600 to help meet the costs of war. Some elaborate mountings still appeared after this time, but the great age of mounted artefacts had virtually ended.

Seville Gates

ABOVE:

The vast grille in Seville Cathedral has two horizontal bands of rectangular panels containing scrollwork, decorative motifs, angels and portraits of saints and Christ.

RIGHT:

A fine late-18th-century wrought-iron railing from a French balcony, now in the Victoria and Albert Museum.

OPPOSITE:

This 'Armada chest' from Nuremberg is made in painted wrought iron and dates from the 16th century. It is housed in the Victoria and Albert Museum.

The magnificent gilded wrought-iron choir screen in Seville Cathedral was made in about 1530 by Sancho Muñoz de Cuenca, assisted by Brother John and Brother Francis of Salamanca. It is decorated with figures and scrollwork and crowned with tall, flame-like finials. The cathedral would have to be large to house such a screen; it is in fact one of the largest churches in the world.

Iron has been worked since prehistoric times, and was considered a precious, magical material in early times. Its two basic forms are wrought iron and cast iron, wrought iron being much the older; cast iron was not developed until about 1400. The earliest uses for wrought iron were purely functional: weapons and simple tools, then nails and door hinges. Gradually, ironwork became more ornamental and, by the 11th century, plain flat strips were being worked into scrolls. By the 12th century, ironwork had become an art form. Screens and grilles were commissioned for churches, sometimes to protect important altars or monuments. During the Renaissance the finest ironwork was produced in Italy, Spain and Germany.

The fibrous structure of wrought iron allows it to be shaped decoratively by hammering, squeezing, rolling or bending. Most of the work is done while the iron is red hot, but some shaping is possible while the metal is cold. The sheer brilliance of the Spanish smiths is shown in their combination of hot-metal forging and benchwork (or locksmithery), the shaping of cold metal by means of hammers and chisels, saws, drills, files and punches. Welding two pieces of wrought iron together is possible if the iron is heated to 1350°C and then hammered.

The scroll, which can be seen in both the screen and the German coffer illustrated, was a

common feature of wrought iron work. A smith would achieve this by wrapping hot metal around a 'scroll former'. Holes could be punched by placing iron over a 'pritchel hole' in an anvil or over one of the holes in a swage block, a tool used in cold-working, and hammering a punch through it. A heated bar could be twisted by holding one end in a vice and then turning it with a wrench.

A great innovation in ironmaking came in 1709 when Abraham Darby of Coalbrookdale perfected the process of coke-smelting. Coal replaced charcoal as the most important fuel, and cast iron came to be used for producing a variety of items, such as decorative benches. These were sometimes fashioned along the same lines as their wrought iron forerunners.

BERLIN IRON JEWELLERY

Cast iron was used to produce delicate, openwork patterned jewellery during the early 19th century. The first factory to make this was the Royal Berlin Factory, founded in 1804, which produced most of the jewellery manufactured in Berlin between 1813 and 1815. There was a scarcity of gold and silver due to the Napoleonic Wars, and this prompted a campaign to collect precious metal from the public. The state offered simple iron jewellery in exchange, and people were urged to be patriotic and give up their gold and silver to help the war effort.

Inscriptions such as 'Gold gab ich für Eisen' (I gave gold for iron) were made on the face of the items, with a portrait of Frederick William III of Prussia on the reverse. The production of cast-iron brooches, necklaces, bracelets, fans, combs and other items continued until the end of the century. Some pieces were made of mesh, using very fine strands of wire.

91

Schlusselfelder Nef

Medieval etiquette placed great importance on a silver gilt vessel marking the place of honour, usually that of the host, at a dinner table. A decorative item in the form of a ship was used for this purpose in France and Germany, much as a great salt-cellar was used in England. Whatever the form of these objects, they were a treasured centrepiece on the High Table. The host and most important guests would dip their meat into a tiny salt container provided somewhere on the nef, while other guests used small salt-cellars.

The Schlusselfelder Nef, a magnificent representation of a ship in silver and parcel-gilt, was made in Nuremberg in about 1503, probably for the patrician Schlusselfelder family, whose descendants now loan it to the Germanisches Nationalmuseum.

By the early 16th century, European rulers were vying with each other in the magnificence of their courts, in patronising the arts and in collecting objects of beauty. Increasing quantities of silver were being mined in Germany, Austria and Hungary and supplies were augmented by mines in India and the Americas. Germany especially was famous throughout Europe for its work in silver and gold, its most important centres being the cities of Augsburg and Nuremberg, which had vibrant metal-working industries. The history of

16th-century German silver is dominated by Wenzel Jamnitzer, who made splendid centrepieces and cups. One of the most distinctive types of vessel produced in Germany at the time was the standing cup and cover, which was intended mainly for display. Pineapple cups, which were shaped like an inverted pineapple on a stem, appeared in the late 16th century and enjoyed their greatest popularity over the next hundred years. Another dining-table feature produced in these centres was the 'Lustbrunnen', or pleasure fountain. This could be quite a complicated object, involving numerous decorative figures and mechanical devices worked by waterpower or clockwork.

The Burghley Nef, another model ship, was made in Paris in about 1482 by Pierre le Flamard and is now housed in London's Victoria and Albert Museum. The base is carved with imitation waves and a siren supports a nautilus shell which forms the hull of the ship. A small depression to hold salt is located in the poop deck at the stern.

By the 18th century these great silver centrepieces were being replaced by a variety of much smaller containers. Small, round three-legged salt-cellars became fashionable in about 1735; these were followed from about 1760 by a version in pierced silver with a blue glass liner. Pepper pots for the dining table first appeared at about the end of the 17th century.

While nefs were decorative, other medieval table objects served a much more practical purpose. A 'proving tree' was a metal standard bearing up to 15 different gemstones on its branching arms. The stones were meant to detect or neutralise any poison that might have been put in meats or wines served at meals. All the royal tables of Europe had at least one proving tree, and these were relied upon to preserve the health and safety of kings and nobles.

Gemstones were dropped one by one into cooked dishes and drinks as they were brought from the kitchen. It was thought that the stones would sweat or change colour if poison were present. As an added insurance, a taster was also employed to sample the food and drink. The main stones used for this purpose were sapphires, rubies and emeralds, but others such as flints, agates and toadstones were used as well, as were sharks' teeth and bezoars.

Armour of Charles IX

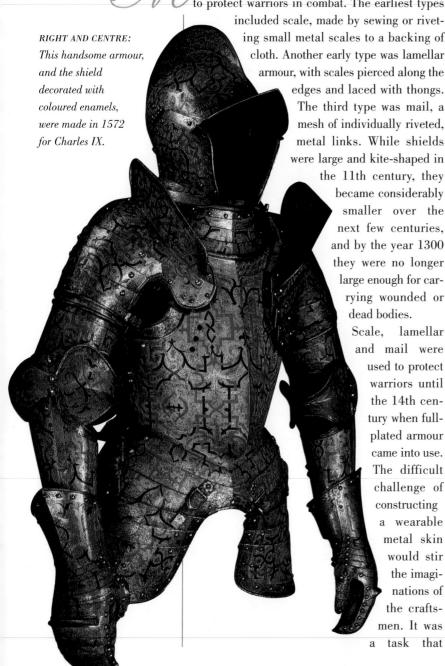

RIGHT AND CENTRE:
This handsome armour,
and the shield
decorated with
coloured enamels,
were made in 1572
for Charles IX.

Metal armour has been used for at least 2,000 years to protect warriors in combat. The earliest types included scale, made by sewing or riveting small metal scales to a backing of cloth. Another early type was lamellar armour, with scales pierced along the edges and laced with thongs. The third type was mail, a mesh of individually riveted, metal links. While shields were large and kite-shaped in the 11th century, they became considerably smaller over the next few centuries, and by the year 1300 they were no longer large enough for carrying wounded or dead bodies.

Scale, lamellar and mail were used to protect warriors until the 14th century when full-plated armour came into use. The difficult challenge of constructing a wearable metal skin would stir the imaginations of the craftsmen. It was a task that required some understanding of human anatomy and, as a suit of armour was custom-made, surviving examples reveal a great deal about body sizes. Those at the Tower Armouries in London give a picture of the changing shape of King Henry VIII. His young 35-in (87-cm) waist grew to a mighty 54in (135cm) in later life.

In 15th- and 16th-century Europe the greatest centre of armour-making was Milan, and the kings of France and Spain, as well as the dukes of Italy, all turned to Milan for custom-made protective suits. Several German cities, including Augsburg, also constructed fine armour. Besides being used in combat, metal armour was worn in jousting tournaments and in parade displays. Splendid parade armour, made for Charles IX of France in 1572 by the Parisian goldsmith Pierre Redon, shows how much attention was lavished on military regalia. The richly enamelled gold shield shown, together with the matching morion (helmet) and armour, is now in the Musée du Louvre in Paris. The items are made of solid gold with richly embossed and engraved decoration enhanced by translucent enamelling. In the centre of the shield is a lively battle scene, and the strapwork pattern includes trophies, cannons and even bound captives.

While highly decorative, the armour of Charles IX had a serious protective purpose as well. After the death of Henry II in 1559, the power of the monarchy weakened and a state of perpetual crisis prevailed until the end of the century. Fontainebleau had been fortified by Charles IX, and became his favourite residence and the main centre of French artistic activity until well into the 17th century. As firearms came into use, armour ceased to be worn in combat. The first important battle won using hand firearms was at fought at Bicocca, near Milan, in 1522, and from that date on the wearing of armour in warfare began to decline. By the end of the century, armour had to be so heavy to offer effective protection against musket shot that it became unwearable. By the 17th century, jousting tournaments were also in decline, and the grandest days of full body armour were over.

RIGHT:

The King's crown monogram displaying the letter 'K' appears on the rim of the shield of Charles IX.

THE MUSÉE DU LOUVRE, PARIS

With its varied and important collections of paintings, sculptures, engravings, drawings, tapestries, ivories, porcelains, gems, terracottas and bronzes, the Musée du Louvre in Paris is one of the great treasure houses of the world. The present buildings stand on the site of a fortress erected by Philip-Augustus in about 1190 and reconstructed in the 13th century by King Charles V. It now occupies an impressive 45 acres (18ha). The modern structure was started as early as 1541. The Sun King, Louis XIV, had the main buildings around the great square erected during the course of his reign (1643–1715) and added considerably to the royal collections. In 1678 he moved to Versailles and the palace of the Louvre then languished for some years; rooms were even occupied by poor Parisians seeking shelter. In the mid-18th century the royal palace was gradually transformed into an ordered museum; the doors first opened to the public in 1793.

Cap of Kazan

The Kremlin houses some of the most complete and spectacular royal regalia in the world. In addition to coaches, thrones and other items, the Armoury

ABOVE, RIGHT AND BELOW:
The covers of three
magnificent copies of the
Book of the Holy
Gospels, dating
respectively from
the 12th, the
15th and the
18th centuries,
now displayed in
the Kremlin
Museum.

maintains a very special collection of crowns. Unlike revolutionaries in England and France, the Bolsheviks believed that regalia from the Tsars of Russia should be preserved. The oldest crown in the collection is probably that of Vladimir II Monomakh (1053–1125), who was Grand Duke of Kiev. The eight panels are decorated with filigree and cabochon stones.

One of the most beautiful crowns in the Kremlin's rich treasury is the Cap, or Crown, of Kazan which was commissioned by Tsar Ivan

IV to commemorate his 1552 victory over Tartars on the Volga. Ivan's reign was one of great excesses in the decorative arts as well as appalling extremes of brutality. His mental instability led to acts of great cruelty, which in turn prompted the adoption of his legendary soubriquet 'Ivan the Terrible'. An example of his savagery involved two architects who designed the cathedral of St Basil the Blessed in Moscow. When the cathedral was finished in 1560, Ivan was so delighted with the result that he ordered the eyes of both architects to be put out so that they could never produce anything better.

The eight gold-leaf spires and central jewel-tipped spire on the cap of Kazan mirror the design of St Basil's Cathedral. The cap has a sable rim and a peaked dome, which was typical of the 'shapka' (cap or hat) worn by the rulers of medieval Russia. While richly ornamented with pure Persian turquoises and Eastern rubies, it is notably lacking in diamonds. Ivan apparantly disliked diamonds and prohibited their use in his State regalia.

Ivan the Terrible made a positive contribution to Russian artistry by establishing workshops in the Kremlin to produce jewelled gifts for monasteries and cathedrals. In 1571 he gave the Book of the Holy Gospels to the Annunciation Cathedral. Its magnificient silver cover is enamelled and embedded with precious stones: giant rubies, sapphires and topazes.

After Ivan's death in 1584 (despite his murderous past, he died in holy orders) the workshops he had established continued to thrive. Gems were generally set in deep mounts and stones were cabochon-cut, although by the mid-17th century, the time of Peter the Great, faceting had been introduced. The stunning Cap of Monomakh, a sable-bordered cap made in 1682–4 with gold plates bearing jewels and pearls, demonstrates the skill of Russian craftsmen in this technique. While early crowns in the Kremlin are designed in the cap style with gold and jewelled domes, later crowns are more like a bishop's mitre in shape. The most splendid regalia was created for the coronation of Catherine the Great in 1762; her crown was set with over 5,000 precious stones.

BELOW:
A giant ruby finial on the dome of the Cap of Kazan was replaced in 1627 by a canary-yellow topaz.

TOPAZ

The topaz is generally yellow – as on the dome of the Cap of Kazan – but it can be found in a wide range of other shades, from pale blue, pale green and pink to golden brown, and even in a colourless form. It is a very hard stone but can break easily. It has been widely used since the 18th century. Gem-quality stones can be found almost all over the world.

Much folk wisdom and superstition has been associated with the topaz. The yellow coloration has marked it as a healing stone for jaundice, and in ancient times a falcon engraved on a topaz was thought to ensure the wearer close ties with the rich and powerful.

The Canning Jewel

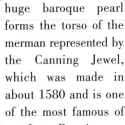

A huge baroque pearl forms the torso of the merman represented by the Canning Jewel, which was made in about 1580 and is one of the most famous of Late Renaissance treasures. The merman's head is gold, his face and arms are enamelled in white and his tail is deco-rated with a range of coloured enamels set with rubies and dia-monds. In his left hand he carries an openwork shield, which is also enamelled and set with stones, and in his right hand he holds a scimi-tar. A cluster of rubies and three irregularly shaped baroque pearls are suspended from the jewel as pendants, in a style very typical of 16th-century designs.

Legend suggests that the Canning Jewel may have been a magnificent offering from a Medici prince to a Mogul emperor. Whatever its exact European origins and the reason for which it was made, the jewel evidently remained in India for a period, since it was there that the carved ruby was placed in the belly, and the ruby and pearl pen-dant was added below. The treasure was acquired in Delhi in the late 1850s by Earl Canning (hence its name), who was Governor-General and Viceroy

of India. It then passed to the first Marquess Clanricarde and later to Viscount Lascelles. After becoming Earl of Harewood, Lascelles sold it in 1931 through Sotheby's auction house in London. The Canning Jewel was bought by Mrs Edward Harkness for the sum of £10,000 and presented to London's Victoria and Albert Museum, where it is kept today.

Irregular baroque pearls were used to great imaginative effect in jewellery of the late 16th century, often representing parts of the human anatomy or the body of some animal. The minute but elaborate pendants of which they formed a

ABOVE:

An enamelled gold pendant made in Paris in about 1540, in which the torso of Hercules is formed from a large irregular baroque pearl.

ABOVE RIGHT:

A baroque pearl represents the body of a cock in this 16th-century Italian jewel.

part displayed the immense technical skill of the craftsmen of the time; these pendants were produced widely in Europe during the Renaissance. Modelling in full relief, using gold, enamel, rubies, emeralds and diamonds as well as pearls, was employed to depict mythological or biblical scenes, monsters, dragons, birds, sailing ships and even miniature architectural compositions, complete with arches, pillars and niches for figures. The production of these continued until the beginning of the 17th century.

Pearls have been credited with special powers over the ages, such as efficacy in treating heart complaints. Dissolving them in lemon juice or crushing them in milk was believed to be a cure for insanity, and in Classical Rome the pearl was an essential ingredient of love potions – hence Cleopatra's toast to Antony with liquid containing a dissolved pearl. During the 16th century, women believed that wearing pearls helped to improve their complexions, and this undoubtedly encouraged the jewel's growing popularity. It was not until the mid-16th century, however, that pearls arrived in great quantities in Europe from India and China. Queen Elizabeth I of England was especially enamoured of them and even had small round pearls sewn on her dresses.

ABOVE:
The whole delicately balanced Canning Jewel is less than 3in (1.5cm) long.

Polish Szkofia

J ewelled ornaments for the hair and hat grew in popularity from the end of the 14th century. During the Renaissance, women wore gold mesh nets over their hair, which were frequently set with elaborate twists of pearls and gems. Men too would adorn themselves with a range of headgear and jewellery such as, for example, the 'szkofia', an ornament worn by Polish men on the left side of their headdress. The delicate example illustrated here dates from the late 16th century and was worn by the Polish king.

In the 13th to 15th centuries badges were made in large numbers by European pilgrimage churches and monasteries and were given or sold to pilgrims visiting the shrines of saints or martyrs. Such badges

MAIN PICTURE:
The Polish royal szkofia was made of silver-gilt combined with turquoises, almandines, pearls and filigree. It is now housed in the National Museum in Kraców.

INSET:
This mid-15th century gold brooch, with enamel decoration en ronde bosse, is set with a ruby, a diamond and pearls.

were generally attached to a pin so that they could be worn on a pilgrim's hat as a sign that he or she had made a visit; afterwards they served as good luck charms. A pilgrim badge was usually made of lead or pewter, but some were made in gold or silver for the nobility.

In the 16th century 'enseignes', which evolved from these pilgrim badges, became one of the most fashionable items of jewellery for men. These were usually decorated with mythological or biblical themes or with portraits of patron saints. While some were worn on the underside of the upturned rim of a hat, many had pierced holes or loops so that they could be sewn to a headdress. Enseignes were often made of gold and surmounted with either enamelled decoration or with an inlaid cameo, as in the case of the Italian badge shown opposite.

The flamboyance of male jewellery (which included earrings, brooches,

pendants, necklaces and rings as well as enseignes) is shown in the portraits of the time. Henry VIII wore more jewels than any of his wives and owned literally hundreds of rings. The brim of his hat was always adorned with a splendid array of colourful jewels.

After the 1570s enseignes declined in popularity and were replaced by 'aigrettes'. These were gold or silver hat or hair ornaments that supported a feather or were made in the form of a plume; they were often covered with designs executed in tiny gemstones. Aigrettes were fashionable from the 17th to late 18th centuries, and came back into vogue in the late 19th and early 20th centuries. Great attention was paid to head ornaments in the 1890s, when glittering hair pins decorated with a feather, an insect, (such as a bee or dragonfly) or a flower motif became extremely popular. Several aigrettes were often worn together, either in the hair or on a hat.

ALMANDINE AND OTHER GARNETS

The almandine on the Polish ornament is actually a variety of deep crimson garnet with a purplish tinge. When cut en cabochon it is often called a 'carbuncle'. The main sources of these stones are Sri Lanka, Alaska and India, where they are shaped by a process called 'tumbling'. This technique involves spinning the stone in a revolving barrel filled with water and using an abrasive and then a polishing powder. It was used in ancient times and became even more common in the 1500s, when the faceting of stones was first introduced, and throughout the following century.

Garnets were widely used by the Egyptians, Greeks, Romans and Celts. They were often cut into thin slices and inlaid, as in cloisonné inlay.

German Tablet Sundial

The 1597 German pocket sundial now in the Science Museum, London, is a fine example of the kind of non-mechanical devices which provided the earliest means of time-keeping. While this sundial used rectangles of brass, most other portable examples of the time used ivory.

Its origin is uncertain, but clockwork time-pieces may have been invented in the Islamic

RIGHT:

This gilt metal folding tablet sundial, now in London's Science Museum, was made in Germany in 1597. It indicates Italian hours, Babylonian hours, planetary or Jewish hours and the sun's place in the ecliptic.

INSET:

A German table clock, dating from 1575–1600, in a circular brass-gilt canister case with engraved hour figures and a central sun.

OPPOSITE ABOVE:

A Japanese clock with adjustable numerals to allow for the Japanese system of timekeeping before 1870: the day and night were each divided into six parts, which changed according to the seasons of the year.

OPPOSITE BELOW:

This drum clock was made in Nuremberg in about 1590.

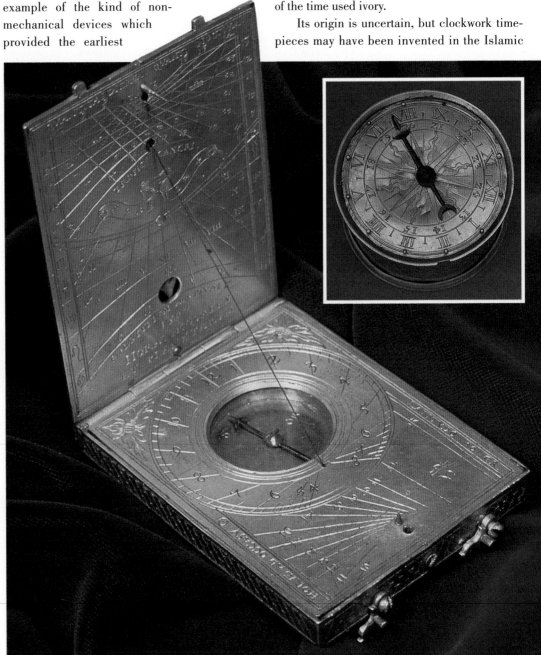

world and spread to the European continent during the 11th century. The earliest examples were made of iron, with a bell to strike the hours. Small markings on the motion wheel and a fixed pointer were used to show the hour, dials being added later.

Clocks were originally made by blacksmiths under the supervision of monks, who were the main users of timepieces. By the 14th century large clocks had begun to appear on churches, palaces and other major buildings in Europe. The earliest domestic clocks were also made of iron and some struck the quarter hour as well as the hour. The first examples appeared in Italy, and were designed to be hung on a hook or to stand on a wall bracket.

Until the 14th century in Europe (and the late 19th century in Japan) daylight and night-time hours were of different lengths, and both varied with the seasons. The period of daylight from dawn to dusk and the period of darkness were each divided into six equal hours. Early clocks were skilfully made to allow for these differences.

In the 16th century clockmaking became a major industry in southern Germany, and Peter Henlein's invention of the spring marked one of several important stages in its development. The first spring-driven clocks were horizontal, the cases being either drum-shaped or square. Another significant change was the introduction of brass as a replacement for iron in the making of cases. It was Nuremberg craftsmen who made the earliest portable watches – miniature, spring-driven mechanisms housed in spherical cases which were worn suspended by a cord from a belt or around the neck.

The 1657 introduction of the pendulum in Holland revolutionised the production of clocks and made more accurate time-keeping possible. Until this time few clocks had been accurate to within a quarter of an hour. The minute hand was not incorporated until after the mid-17th century, and a pendulum beating at intervals of exactly one second was then developed. As the use of brackets gradually diminished, clocks were placed centrally on a mantlepiece and came to be known as mantle clocks.

By the early 18th century, clockmaking was becoming an established industry in the United States, where most clocks were of the longcase kind with a brass eight-day movement. Longcase clocks, which dated from about 1670 in England, were often decorated with elaborate designs in marqetry, and inlaid with brass and other metals.

WATCHES

The invention of the spring-driven clock led to the development of the pocket watch, which was first made in Europe in the 16th century. The most significant early centres of watchmaking were Nuremberg in Germany and Blois in France, but Paris and Geneva took the lead in the 17th century and still maintain it to this day. While early pocket watches were spherical, the more familiar flat, circular case soon appeared. By the early 17th century watches sometimes included alarms and even calendars. The decoration lavished on some, which incorporated enamel paintings, inset pearls and superb engraving on dials and backplates – cases were often made of gold or silver – made them works of art. Queen Elizabeth I and the Empress Josephine had wristwatches, but these came into general use only after 1850.

Venetian Wedding Mirror

OPPOSITE:

The frame of this Venetian wedding mirror is made of gold, cameos, precious jewels and semiprecious stones set in the Italian pietra dura style. It is now housed in the Louvre in Paris.

RIGHT:

In the Jewish wedding ceremony the groom placed the 16th-century cupola ring on the middle finger of the bride's right hand. Such a ring was simply set aside thereafter and not worn, though it was often preserved by the family or the synagogue congregation.

The Venetian Renaissance reached its fullest flowering in the second half of the 15th century, about half a century later than in Florence and taking a somewhat different form. As well as the great painters who produced some of the finest work of the age in Venice, a profusion of talented craftsmen also gathered there, turning out fine work in gems, metals, enamels, textiles, jewellery and leather.

Venice at that time was a city of great wealth and power. In the late 15th century one traveller wrote 'it is impossible to tell or write fully of the beauty, the magnificence or the wealth of the city'. Venice's prosperity grew steadily in the 16th century, mainly as a result of her profits in sea trade and the riches of the empire she controlled. This was a golden age, when Venetian confidence was high and even her rivals conceded her grudging admiration.

The superb mirror illustrated is a splendid example of Venetian artistry. It dates from about 1600 and was given by the Venetian Republic to Marie de' Medici as a wedding gift. Another treasure from this illustrious city is a 16th-century silver and pearl Jewish wedding ring. It incorporates a model of a building with a cupola, symbolising the marital home, and has a Hebrew inscription intended to bring good luck to the bride and groom. Some examples of such rings have a pierced window and a high gabled roof, and

even a movable weather vane on top. The wedding ring shown is now housed in the Ashmolean Museum in Oxford.

Rings assumed much importance during the Renaissance, and in the 16th century were elaborately decorated. Rich ornamentation with pierced work, niello (see page 71) and enamel was common. Many had bezels which opened to reveal a small portrait or other memento. A popular wedding ring in Italy was the 'gimmel' ring, made of two divisible hoops of plain gold. Sometimes these took the form of hands painted in enamel; when the two rings were united the hands were shown interlocked. Engagement rings of the period often had bezels in the shape of hearts set with gems.

A famous example of a jewel believed to have been made to mark a marriage is the 'AA pendant', a gold pendant with enamelling and diamonds forming the monogram 'AA', above which is a crown set with rubies. The pendant is thought to have been presented in 1546 to Anna, the daughter of Christian II of Denmark, on her wedding to the future Elector Augustus I of Saxony. The monogram combined their initials. This jewel was made in either Munich or Augsburg and is now housed in the Green Vault (Grünes Gewölbe) in Dresden.

Koh-i-noor Diamond

The Koh-i-noor Diamond – the name means 'mountain of light' – is one of Britain's most famous royal jewels. While not the largest diamond in the world, nor even the most valuable, its colourful history has given the Koh-i-noor enormous mystique and status. The changing fortunes of the gem have been linked to the history of the subcontinent of India, where it was found over 300 years ago.

Since its discovery in 1655, in a mine in Andhra Pradesh, the Koh-i-noor has been passed around from conqueror to

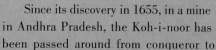

conqueror. With the sacking of Delhi by Nadir Shar in
1739, the diamond acquired its current name. It was taken
to Isfahan in Persia (now Iran) and in 1751, having been
inherited by Nadir's grandson in 1747, the Koh-i-noor was
passed to Ahmad Shah Durran in northern Persia. It was
then moved to Kabul, the capital of Afghanistan, and there it
remained until 1813, when Shah Shuja surrendered it to
Rajit Singh in Lahore.

With the annexation of the Punjab in 1849, the
diamond was claimed by the British. It sailed to
England from India in an iron-bound casket that was
enclosed in an outer chest. For added security, each
box was double-locked and the keys were conscien-
tiously guarded by two different people. The Koh-i-noor
travelled from Bombay to the Cape of Good Hope, to
Portsmouth and finally to London for presentation to
Queen Victoria on 3 July 1850.

Many of the six million people who came to
London's Great Exhibition of 1851 came especially
to view 'the finest diamond, the finest ruby and the
finest emerald' known in the world, and they
gasped in admiration at what they saw. The
Queen of Spain's jewels were displayed at
the exhibition, along with some of the
Russian crown jewels.

In 1852, the Koh-i-noor was
entrusted to Garrard's, London's famous
jewellers, and an expert cutter was
brought over from Amsterdam. The Koh-i-
noor was cut as a 'rose', which has a flatter
base than a brilliant cut, and the delicate
work took him 38 days. (The rose-cut style,
developed by Dutch lapidaries in the mid-17th
century, lost some popularity when the brilliant
style was invented in the early 18th century.)

When British sovereignty over India dissolved
in 1947, Indians began to argue that the Koh-i-noor
should be returned to them. The question of ownership
was brought up again in 1953, to be greeted by a
prolonged protest in the British press that the
diamond should stay in England; it had clearly
become an important emotional symbol for
Britain as well as for India. The wider debate
about treasures of the world being returned to
their original sources was revived, and the con-
troversy is likely to continue for some years yet.

RIGHT:
An important part of the British Crown Jewels,
the highly ornate King's Sceptre with the Cross
features the magnificent Star of Africa
diamond.

Dutch Wagering Cup

O rnate silverwork, as shown on the wall sconce illustrated, was a speciality of the Netherlands in the 17th century. The van Vianen brothers, Paul and Adam, were born in Utrecht in the mid-1560s and were celebrated especially for their embossed and chased silverware. The elaborate designs called 'Kwabornament' for which they were known were forerunners of the rococo style. In the early 1600s Paul went to Prague to become court goldsmith to Rudolf II, Emperor of the Holy Roman Empire and noted patron of the arts (see page 116).

The Dutch love of flowers became evident in silver patterns from the mid-17th century onwards, when representations of tulips were chased on dishes, ewers and other articles. Up to the end of the 16th century there was little difference between the styles of Dutch and German silverware – but the distinct style which emerged in Holland in the 17th century was admired throughout Europe.

Some of the articles made by Dutch silversmiths had uses which were specific to the Netherlands. A 'brandy bowl' was a rounded or hexagonal two-handled drinking vessel filled with brandy and raisins for 17th- and 18th-century family gatherings. The bowls often had engravings depicting family life.

A distinctively Dutch windmill cup included a charming miniature windmill perched on an inverted wine cup. Incorporated into the design was a tube through which the drinker, having

RIGHT:

A single-light sconce in the Anglo-Dutch Restoration style dating from 1668–90.

OPPOSITE, INSET:

A spectacular piece of silverware known as the Dolphin Dish. It was made in about 1685 by Christian van Vianen who carried on the tradition established by his ancestors, Paul and Adam van Vianen, over a century earlier.

upended the cup and filled it with wine, was required to blow in order to turn the sails of the mill. He then had to empty the cup before the sails stopped. If he failed he had to start again.

In Holland a wagering cup was known as a 'bridal cup' as it was often used to drink a toast at weddings. It was made in the image of a woman – her long skirt taking the form of a large, fixed cup – with a smaller, pivoted bowl swinging in a cradle over her head. The figure was turned upside down and both cup and bowl were filled with wine. The drinker had first to drink the wine from the 'skirt', then reverse the cup and empty the smaller bowl without spilling a drop.

Another distinctive Dutch cup was called 'Hansje in den Kelder' (Hans in the cellar). It was brought out to celebrate news that a child was expected. Under a domed lid in the centre, a figure of a baby popped up when the vessel was filled with wine. These were popular from the 16th to 19th centuries. There were also silver-gilt stands for holding wine glasses, and goblets made from coconut shells which were carved and polished, then mounted in silver or silver-gilt.

EMBOSSING AND CHASING

Dutch craftsmen of the 17th century excelled at embossing and chasing, a technique that raised the decoration above the surface of the object. The cast ingot was first flattened, leaving it to thicken in areas requiring a deeply-etched design. The pattern was then embossed or punched up from the underside while it was held against a bed of soft lead or pitch. It was neatened on the outside using a blunt chasing instrument.

Chasing indents the design

RIGHT:
A wagering or 'bridal cup' made by John Angell and dating from 1827. Once the figure has been upended, the cup formed by the woman's skirt and the bowl swinging over her head are both filled with wine to toast the newly married couple at a wedding feast.

from the front but, unlike engraving, does not remove any metal. When used for a pattern on a flat surface it is known as 'flat chasing'.

Pietra Dura Table

Artists of the Italian Renaissance were often subsidised and encouraged by powerful noble families and wealthy merchants. The most famous Florentine ruling family were the Medici, who dominated Florence and later much of Tuscany for most of the period from 1434 to 1737. Only two brief intervals (1494–1512 and 1527–30) interrupted this reign. Originally from peasant stock, the Medici provided four popes and married into the royal families of Europe, most notably France.

As patrons of the arts the greatest among them were Lorenzo 'the Magnificent' (1449–92) and Cosimo (1389–1464).

The fine Medici palace became the cultural and artistic centre of Florence, a meeting place for both artists and scholars. Splendid festivals and pageants were held in the city, with scenery, costumes and processional floats designed by artists of the Medici circle.

A special academy was established in Florence to encourage the study of Greco-Roman art. This revived interest in classical art and philosophy during the Renaissance and led to the foundation of the Humanist movement in which Lorenzo de Medici was a central figure. While religion was still Christian, a much freer, more natural spirit evolved than had existed in medieval times.

In the late 15th century a fanatical preacher, Savonarola, led a revolt against Humanism, which was seen by some people as pagan, and in 1497 many great artistic treasures and jewels were heaped in a pile and burned. Lorenzo de' Medici had died and the people of Florence expelled his heirs – but within decades the Medici were again a powerful force in Florentine art and politics.

The Medici Vase by Bernardo Buontalenti and Giovanni Bilivert is an elegant example of the many objects using semiprecious stones, such as lapis, onyx and chalcedony, which were commissioned by the great Italian patrons of the 16th century. Italian decorative art has continued to feature a variety of inlaid mosaics using cut and polished stones in a technique called 'pietra dura', combining such materials as amethyst, lapis lazuli, onyx, agate and jasper in motifs which often include flowers, birds and butterflies. Pietra dura was well developed by the 16th century and often

THE SACRIFICE OF ISAAC

The Sacrifice of Isaac, now housed in the Museo Nazionale, Florence, is a small relief bronze plaque which was made in 1401 by the great sculptor Lorenzo Ghiberti (1378–1455). When the city council of Florence decided to commission two new doors for the cathedral baptistry it held a competition for the work. Ghiberti submitted *The Sacrifice of Isaac* and won the commission. He spent the next 21 years working on the doors and the rest of his life creating another pair, the magnificent *Gates of Paradise*. The Ghiberti doors are among Florence's major treasures and are celebrated as masterpieces of the Early Italian Renaissance.

incorporated a rich variety of further materials such as inlays of ivory, exotic woods, mother-of-pearl, shells and various metals. Cabinets and other furniture made in this style were frequently fitted with gilded bronze mounts.

The finest pietra dura was produced in the 17th century, when every stylish home in Italy and much of Europe had at least one item featuring the technique. The octagonal table illustrated here is the work of two of the greatest Italian masters of the art of pietra dura, Jacopo Ligozzi and Bernardino Poccetti. It is inlaid with agates, jaspers, lapis lazuli and chalcedonies on a black marble ground. Much of the furniture in the French royal court incorporated pietra dura mosaic, often highly ornamented with gilded metal and wood.

Caudle Cups

RIGHT:

Animated scenes showing the hunting of deer and wild boar cover the surface of the Ashley-Cooper caudle cup and salver. Made in silver-gilt in about 1665, these two fine pieces can now be seen in the Victoria and Albert Museum.

drink of warm wine or ale mixed with bread or gruel, eggs, sugar and spices, first introduced in the 14th century, became especially popular in Europe in the 17th century. This revitalising 'caudle' was often given to women after childbirth and to convalescents, and two-handled cups called 'caudle cups' were made to hold the brew. The domed lid of the cup sometimes had a flat finial which allowed it to be reversed and used as a stand.

Caudle cups, also known as porringers, came in a variety of shapes and sizes.

Throughout the period from the 14th to the 19th century they were made in pewter. In the 17th and 18th centuries caudle cups were also produced in silver and silver-gilt and, from the mid-18th century, in Sheffield plate. German examples often had three feet and were slightly deeper than those made in England. In America they had pierced handles to enable them to be hung.

Another item linked to the growing use of spices in Europe was the pomander (from the French *pomme d'ambre* meaning amber apple). These small, spherical metal containers held balls of aromatic spices or herbs prepared by an apothecary or perfumer, and would have been worn around the neck or at the waist to counteract the evil smells that were an ever-present part of life in the Middle Ages. Pomanders were often enriched with gems and enamels and became fashionable as items of jewellery. In the 16th century the sphere was divided into segments, as can be seen in the example illustrated, which has six labelled compartments designed to hold a variety of aromatic substances. These usually included ambergris – a waxy substance with a musk-like odour from the intestines of whales – spices such as cinnamon, herbs, musk and civet. General fear of disease was another reason for wearing pomanders, and plague treatises strongly recommended their use. It was thought that frequent smelling of aromatic compounds would help ward off airborne infections. In a 17th-century variation of the pomander apothecaries used aromatic ammonia, which was made by distilling the shavings of stags' horns. Fragrant oils were mixed with the ammonia. Double-ended smelling-salts bottles, some with gold or silver caps, became fashionable in the 19th century.

Pomanders were succeeded in the 18th and 19th centuries by the vinaigrette, which was usually chased or engraved. The gold or silver gilt case had a pierced inner grid to hold a piece of sponge soaked in aromatic vinegar. Its function was similar to that of a pomander; it would be sniffed by ladies who were feeling faint.

LEFT:
A silver-gilt pomander decorated with chased scrollwork enclosing black enamel. It dates from about 1580 and is the property of the London silversmiths and jewellers Asprey and Co.

BELOW:
This French gold pomander, dating from c1600, has late Renaissance enamelled decoration set with stones. It is divided into segments, each one containing an aromatic spice or fragrance.

THE SPICE TRADE

Spices such as cinnamon, cassia, cardamom, ginger and turmeric were already being used by Eastern cultures thousands of years ago to flavour food and help in preserving it.

By the 13th century much of Venice's great wealth came from trading in spices from India, Ceylon, the East Indies and Cathay (the archaic name for China), and the 15th-century voyages of discovery were largely prompted by other regions of Europe wanting to find cheaper sources for themselves. Dutch ships returned from the East with rich cargoes of cloves, mace, nutmeg and pepper. In 1600 England formed the East India Company to trade in the East Indies, which it continued to do until the dissolution of the Company in 1874.

TRADITIONAL CRAFTS

Delicate inlay was a feature of Japanese 'inros'. Made mainly of lacquered wood in the form of an oblong box, they were generally lacquered in black and red, with inlaid scenes in gold and mother-of-pearl. The word 'inro' literally means 'seal case', and the earliest examples in Japan and China were used for holding seals or an ink pad and were kept on a shelf at home. In about 1500 the inro developed into a flattish, rectangular box with three to six compartments, to be carried with a net-suke (see page 132) on a kimono sash. These portable inros were widely used by Japanese men as handy carrying cases for smoking and writing equipment until about the 1870s.

A running bead called an ojime was used to keep the sections of the inro in place. These ojime, which were highly decorative, were usually made of carved wood, coral, cloisonné, semiprecious stones, porcelain or sometimes even gold.

TORTOISESHELL

Despite its name, tortoiseshell is not a shell but an organic material derived from the overlapping horny plates on the upper shell of turtles. The preferred source has been the hawksbill turtle, found off the West Indies and Brazil, and the loggerhead turtle, found near the Celebes in Eastern Indonesia. The translucent plates are dark brown in colour, marbled with a yellowish tinge. Since Roman times tortoiseshell has been used for inlay work and for making personal items such as combs and jewellery, including cameos. The Romans also used it as a furniture veneer. Tortoiseshell was put to various decorative uses from the early 17th century in Germany and the Low Countries, and became popular in 17th- and 18th-century France and England where it was especially associated with inlay and marquetry work (see page 118). Conservation concerns has encouraged the use of tortoiseshell substitutes, such as celluloid and stained horn, which are now frequently used to imitate it.

BELOW:
A Japanese inro showing a servant kneeling before a Samurai, signed by Jitokusai Gyokuzan

EAST MEETS WEST

Somewhat similar to these Japanese boxes were the ornate
European snuff boxes of the 18th century (see pages 126–7).
By the mid-18th century snuff boxes were turning into small
picture galleries – much like the boxes illustrated here – the
enamelled miniature paintings which by now adorned them
set off by elaborate gold frames.

ABOVE, FROM TOP:
A tobacco pouch with
Hiramaki-e design, signed
Zeshin; an inro showing a
foxes' wedding procession,
signed Toyo; an inro
with two sages reading a scroll
in Sumi-e Togidashi, signed
Kanshosai

ABOVE AND TOP:
Two Japanese inros
executed in Togidashi,
one with a scene of
boating on a lake, the
other with a duck

LEFT:
A late-18th to 19th century
Japanese inro in lacquered
wood, coral and shell with
pine, bamboo and plum
decoration

Rudolf Crown

ROYAL TREASURE

One of the great royal art collectors, Rudolf assembled a massive hoard of artistic treasures, which was housed in Hradcany Palace in Prague until it was dispersed to museums in Vienna, Munich and Stockholm. Vienna's Kunsthistorisches Museum still has many of his treasures, as well as the 17th-century crown of his enemy, the Prince of Transylvania; this splendid gold crown is topped by an emerald and holds a dazzling 188 gems and 214 pearls.

INSET:
The lower part of the Alfred Jewel takes the form of a boar's head. The figure depicted on the panel above has been identified as either Christ, the Pope, Alfred himself or possibly a saint.

Preserved in the Vienna museum is the crown made for Rudolf II as a lighter, more comfortable alternative to the Imperial Crown (see page 58). Rudolf II became Holy Roman Emperor in 1576. He was a great patron of the arts and enjoyed painting as well as polishing and shaping stones in workshops that he established in the grounds of his palace. His craftsmen carved cameos for him out of agate and other stones, and set glorious gems in silver and gold. His fascination with lapidary work may have encouraged his desire to create a new imperial crown.

Rudolf's crown, made in the early 1600s, has a circlet of gold with pavé-set gems butted together like paving stones within borders of pearls. Above the circlet rise eight gem-set *fleurs-de-lis* topped with large pearls. An unusual feature of the crown is that the panels inside the circlet incline towards the centre, rather like a bishop's mitre. These are decorated with borders of enamel depicting birds and flowers. The crown also depicts scenes from Rudolf's somewhat eccentric life, such as the fact that he often took walks through his gardens with a lion call Ottakar, which he had raised from a cub. The crown is finally topped by a high crest, made of plates of gold – which would have made Rudolf appear taller than his 5 feet 5 inches (1.63m). This may have been part of his intention in revising the design of the imperial crown.

An altogether different royal artefact, a tiny tear-shaped panel of enamel, was discovered at Atherney in Somerset in 1693. Protected by a layer of rock crystals, the panel depicts the head and shoulders of a man carrying two sceptres. The whole object is bordered by a delicate collar of gold filigree. An inscription on the side reads 'Aelfred me heht gewyrcan' (Alfred had me made) which is why this treasure is now known as The Alfred Jewel. The item is thought to date from the 9th century and to have been lost by King Alfred the Great while he

ABOVE:
This highly ornate royal object, this time from the Orient, is the Phoenix Coronet, an empress's hair piece from the Ming Dynasty.

was hiding from the Danes in about 878. Alfred became king of Wessex, the south-western region of Anglo-Saxon Britain, in 871 and by 886 he had captured London and was king of all England. The precise purpose of the object remains unclear. It might have been the central jewel of a crown or worn as a brooch or pendant. It might even have been the tip of an 'aestel' pointer for indicating lines in a manuscript. The unusual object is now on display at the Ashmolean Museum in Oxford along with the 9th century Minster Lovel Jewel, which it resembles.

BELOW:
This highly bejewelled crown was made for Rudolf II by Jan Vermeyen in 1602.

Boulle Mirror Back

André-Charles Boulle (1642–1732) was one of the most influential designers in the history of furniture. His use of inlaid tortoiseshell and brass, mother-of-pearl, gold and silver accorded perfectly with the opulent tastes of the aristocracy of the day

ABOVE:
This late 17th-century tortoiseshell tray from France, inlaid with gilt and mother-of-pearl, is now displayed in the Victoria and Albert Museum.

and with the great gilded palaces such as Versailles in which his splendid pieces were housed. The son of a carpenter, Boulle first trained as a painter, and at the age of 30 was commissioned by Louis XIV to produce magnificent furnishings for the royal houses.

Following his retirement, Boulle left his studio to his sons, who included the noted cabinet makers André-Charles II and Charles-Joseph. Unfortunately, the collection was destroyed by a

fire in 1720, revealing a prolific amount of work when these losses were taken into account and added to those pieces of furniture already in other collections. André-Charles senior returned to his studio, directing the work until his death.

Much patience, artistry and care were needed to carry out the technique of brass and tortoiseshell marquetry which he developed, a method now known as Boulle work (or buhl-work), and his unparallelled genius for fine inlay work raised cabinet-making to a superior art form.

The Romans also used tortoiseshell as a furniture veneer, and since ancient times this highly decorative material has been used for inlay work and in the making of personal items such as hair-combs and jewellery, especially cameos.

Gilt-bronze mounts were often added to inlaid furniture, making the objects even more sumptuous. These mounts had a practical as well as a decorative purpose. Applying different metals (silver, brass or pewter) to wood, along with organic substances (horn, ivory, tortoise- shell and mother-of-pearl) meant that veneers were susceptible to warping and distortion. Each material reacted differently to varying conditions of temperature and humidity. The mounts helped to hold pieces together, therefore overcoming the vulnerability of the inlay.

In addition to large pieces of furniture, Boulle also applied his marquetry to smaller objects such as mirror and picture frames, inkstands and jewel caskets. A fine example of his skill is the decorated mirror back illustrated here, which he made for Charlotte de Saint-Simon.

Other notable examples of marquetry can be seen in the work of another Frenchman, Louis Marjorelle (1859–1926), who was also an ironworker and artist, studying under Jean-François Millet. He was a major exponent of art nouveau.

BELOW AND INSET: André-Charles Boulle's early 18th-century inlaid mirror back is the property of the Wallace Collection.

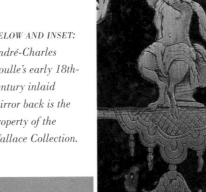

MIRRORS

Highly polished sheets of gold, silver or bronze were used as mirrors from ancient times until the 15th century, early glass being too opaque to reflect an image clearly. The first commercially made plates of mirror glass came from Murano on the Venetian lagoon in about 1500, and the Venetians held the monopoly on mirror manufacture until Flanders and Germany also began production. Glass casting, invented by the French in the late 17th century, made it possible to produce larger and finer mirrors. Mirrors were at first silvered with tin foil and mercury, but by 1840 a German chemist had found a way of chemically depositing real silver on to glass. Mirror–glass making altered little for two centuries, but frames evolved considerably – they became decorative works of art, and in the 18th century were frequently gilded.

Cameo Chatelaine

CENTRE:

This gold chatelaine, from Christie's in London, is decorated with blue enamel and hung with cameos.

RIGHT:

This half-hunter watch might well have been worn suspended on a chatelaine around the waist.

Ornamental clasps called 'chatelaines' first came into use in the 16th century and by the 18th and early 19th centuries had achieved widespread popularity. The clasps were attached at a woman's waist with a hook plate suspending between five and nine short chains holding rings or swivel catches. Small objects for daily use, such as a watch and keys, were carried in this way. Some chatelaines held a small purse, a pincushion, a tape measure, a household notebook, a handkerchief, a pomander and even good luck charms. A small ornamental case called an étui (made in gold, silver or pinchbeck), also designed to be suspended from a chatelaine, served to hold a variety of sharp items such as needles and scissors. Chatelaines made for men tended to be longer and held watches, seals and charms.

A longer version of a chatelaine was called a 'macaroni', which was worn slung over a close-fitting belt or girdle. Its two ends hung down equally, one end holding an ornamental medallion with several small hooks for a watch and other articles, the other a *fausse montre* (literally meaning 'false watch'). This was in fact a case for a small mirror, a pincushion or a vinaigrette. Some *fausses montres* were almost as opulent as real watches and were made of gold or silver with enamelled or jewelled backs.

Another popular fashion in the 18th century was for cut steel, in which beads of soft steel were facet-cut and riveted to a back-plate, creating an effect somewhat like pavé-set diamonds or paste. Cut steel, which was actually a substitute for both stones and metal, was worn even in the highest

LEFT:
An elegant watch in gold and blue enamel

society. In some cases it was more expensive than real jewels. Cut steel jewellery was first made in England in the 1760s and later elsewhere in Europe. After 1759, wealthy people in France were asked to contribute their jewellery to the treasury and wear cut steel jewels instead. It retained its popularity right through to the late 19th century in the decoration of brooches, bracelets, tiaras and necklaces, combs, handbag frames, seals, buttons, rings and hair ornaments.

Buckles of various kinds have been used since Roman times and became especially fashionable in the 18th century. Matthew Boulton, a leading manufacturer of metal objects, designed a number of buckles made of cut steel combined with plaques of jasper. The hard, fine-ground, unglazed stoneware called jasper was introduced by the English ceramic manufacturer Josiah Wedgwood in 1764. The relief decoration on jasper plaques was usually white, imitating the effect of a cameo. Medallions of Wedgwood's jasper were sometimes worn as ornamental pendants on chatelaines as well.

PINCHBECK AND PASTE

Copper may be used pure or in alloys: combined with tin it produces bronze; with zinc it makes brass. Pinchbeck, an alloy of copper and zinc developed in 1720, is much lighter than gold, and was used for items such as chatelaines, watchcases, buckles and clasps. It also met the need for a cheaper material as the desire for jewellery spread to a wider market.

By the mid-17th century the manufacture of artificial precious stones was well established. In 1676 George Ravenscroft invented a way of making 'paste' glass with lead oxide to simulate diamonds. High-quality paste is now made in the former Czechoslovakia, France and Austria.

ABOVE:
This blue-and-white jasper cameo is mounted in cut steel.

RIGHT:
Polished semiprecious stones such as onyx were often used in the making of watch cases for chatelaines.

Polish Wheel Lock Gun

Little is known about the early history of firearms, but gunpowder was certainly used, if on a limited scale, in China in the 11th century before making its way westwards. For some types of firearms a range of accessories is required for operation, and

tem was developed at around the end of the 15th century, but it was very vulnerable to wind and weather. Rain could extinguish the glowing end of the cord, and the wind blew sparks about. Gunsmiths then came up with another improvement, the wheel lock. This mechanical system of ignition was far less vulnerable to the weather than the

RIGHT:

A 17th-century wheel lock gun with decorative inlay, made in southern Poland in now in the Museum im Augustinerstock, Munich.

Islamic gunmakers have always lavished great care and artistry on their design and manufacture. Turkish powder flasks were made in a variety of materials and shapes: some, an example being an 18th-century silver one, took the form of hunting horns. Persian craftsmen often adapted their flasks from nature, as shown by another 18th-century example made from a seashell mounted in silver and decorated with niello (see page 71). Both the Turkish horn and the Persian shell are housed in the collection of London's Victoria and Albert Museum. In the same collection is a rich assembly of smallswords, such as the Swiss example illustrated here, which dates from about 1760.

The first use of firearms in Europe was in the 14th century, the earliest illustration of a crude gun dating from 1326. The matchlock ignition sys-

matchlock, but wheel locks were expensive to produce and were never made on a large scale. While early guns were little more than a plain tube, wheel lock pistols and longarms were often works of art, inlaid with gold and silver, mother-of-pearl and even ivory. Wheel locks were in use from about 1550 to 1650, but a much simpler mechanical system called the flintlock replaced both the wheel lock and the matchlock for common use from the mid-1600s.

New fencing techniques in the latter part of the 17th century encouraged the development of the smallsword. The changed approach involved using the point rather than the edge of the sword, and also required greater speed in attack and defence. The smallsword was a light rapier developed to meet this new need. Two small rings below the guard enable the fencer to manoeuvre the point more easily. Small-swords were worn mainly to complement civilian dress so their decorative features were important. They were in fact an item of male jewellery. Like the elegant boxes which were so fashionable in the 18th century, sword hilts were decorated with different coloured gold alloys. While gold-hilted smallswords were often presented as rewards for gallantry or special services rendered, others were made with silver or steel hilts. These too were often finely embellished. The 18th-century sword cutlers of Tula in Russia were known for their exquisite work in chiselled steel, in which they inlaid gold and silver flowers.

VICTORIA AND ALBERT MUSEUM

London's Victoria and Albert Museum is the world's greatest museum of the decorative arts. Dating from 1852, it is also the oldest museum of its kind. It provided a permanent home to treasures from the Great Exhibition of 1851, and, since moving to South Kensington in 1857, it has accumulated at least a million objects in nine departments. The metalwork department has a wide-ranging collection of gold and silver objects, including jewellery, arms and armour, ironwork, brasswork, pewter and a large number of metal-cased clocks. The collection's greatest benefactor was Dame Joan Evans (1893–1977), a writer on medieval art and jewellery. By 1975 she had loaned a total of 250 objects, which were eventually presented as gifts to the Museum.

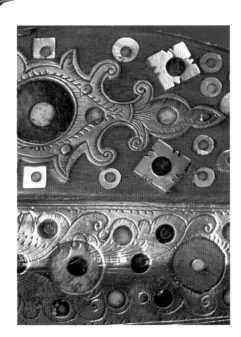

ABOVE:
A detail of the decorative inlay on the Polish wheel lock gun.

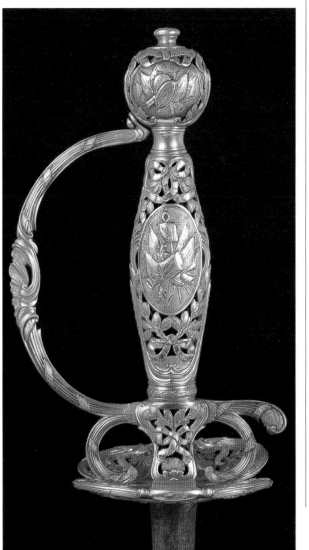

RIGHT:
The hilt of a magnificent 18th-century gold smallsword in the Victoria and Albert Museum.

Louis XV Ormolu Clock

The word 'ormolu' describes a style of intricate gilding employed from the late 17th to 19th centuries. It is mainly associated with France, where the technique was refined in the mid-17th century. Some of its finest exponents had trained in sculpture, and the human figure often featured in the items they created. The most skilled ormolu artists worked for the French royal family.

Ormolu was used on a wide range of objects, from door handles and decorative vases to light fittings and elaborate firedogs known as chenets. It was also used in the mounting of oriental lacquerwork and for embellishing furniture and fine porcelain.

Ormolu objects were cast using the lost-wax method (see page 135) and the metal was pushed into shape by means of a hammer. Various tools were then used to indent and chase the surface. The alloy used to make all these objects varied, but usually contained a large proportion of copper with smaller parts of zinc and sometimes tin. A special feature of all ormolu ware was the surface, which was made golden by the 'fire gilding' or 'mercury gilding' process. The French phrase 'd'orure d'or moulu' means literally 'gilding with gold that has been ground up'.

Clocks were a popular subject for ormolu gilding, and it is fortunate that at least some examples survive. While spring-driven clocks had been made in France as early as the 16th century, few examples from that period still exist; most were taken apart to salvage the precious gold and silver that was used in their decoration.

By the late 17th century and the reign of Louis XIV, ormolu was being used lavishly on clocks and other decorative objects. Many pendulum clocks included elegant tortoiseshell veneers as well as silver and brass inlays. André Charles Boulle (see pages 118–19) fashioned some highly ornate clock cases, combining the careful detail of his marquetry with the bold opulence of ormolu. During the reign of Louis XV (1723–74) clocks were ornamented with rococo scrolls, shells and flowers in ormolu, and porcelain clock cases were provided with elaborate ormolu mounts.

In the late 1700s, during the reign of Louis XVI, popular decorations for

ABOVE:

A detail of the delicate Vincennes porcelain flowers surrounding the Louis XV ormolu clock.

RIGHT:

A French lyre clock made about 1810, in white marble ormolu wreathed with paste jewels.

124

clocks included urns, together with animal and human figures. Bracket and cartel (wall) clocks were being replaced by mantel clocks, including an elegant type in the form of a lyre. With some lyre clocks, the enamel dial was cut away in the centre to show the movement. Ormolu gilding remained popular throughout the 18th century.

France is well known for many elegant and finely made carriage clocks that were produced from the late 18th to the early 20th centuries. These were originally produced mainly for use by military officers while travelling, and were sparsely ornamented compared to the heavily gilded clocks of previous centuries.

LEFT:

The Louis XV chinoiserie clock stands on an ormolu mount supporting tole figures of a Chinese man and a child. It was made by Jacques-Jerome Gudin in the mid-18th century; the later movement is by James Grohe.

CHINOISERIE

The Chinese Manchu or Ch'ing dynasty, founded in 1644, expanded trade with the West and goods began to be made solely for export to European countries. By the late 17th century, European decorative arts had became so inspired by the Orient that European craftsmen were producing objects in a style which came to be known as 'Chinoiserie'. This term embraced a wide range of figures, pagodas, monsters and landscapes made by Europeans in imitation of Chinese style. It was applied mainly to decorative objects rather than jewellery. Exotic motifs based on Japanese, Indian and Turkish art were also adopted by European craftsmen. In the 18th century, the Eastern influence became evident on enamelled porcelain, lacquerware, and other items such as clocks.

INSET:

The panels of this 1780
French box are of lapis lazuli
and the enamelled portrait is
of Marie Antoinette

RIGHT:

A Louis XV oval snuff box in
gold, agate and enamel,
made by Gabriel Gallois of
Paris, in 1738

BELOW:

A Frederick Augustus III
snuff box by Johann
Christian Neuber in
hardstone porcelain and
gold, made in Dresden in
1775

RIGHT:

An openwork gold snuff box
from Denmark, made in
about 1767, with agate
inserts and an enamelled
portrait of Prince Ferdinand
inside the lid

A FRENCH FASHION

Tobacco was known in France by the mid-1550s, but it was a hundred years later before snuff first appeared. The taking of snuff enjoyed a great vogue in late 17th-century France and tiny decorative boxes were produced to contain it. By 1740 snuff boxes were social necessities, lavishly made in gold and precious stones, and used for a variety of purposes: to hold wafers for fastening letters, romantic souvenirs, powder or rouge for the face, or even sweeteners for the breath (see also Japanese Inros, pages 114–15).

Early 18th-century boxes were usually either rectangular or oval but other, more complex, shapes soon appeared, to be followed by boxes in the form of carriages, travelling trunks or even hip baths.

GEMSTONE DECORATION

In 1741 Frederick II forbade the import of French work into Germany, and a different, larger style of snuff box was produced by German craftsmen, often using hard gemstones on the lid. These included colourless quartz and varieties of chalcedony such as agate, cornelian, jasper, bloodstone, heliotrope, onyx and chrysoprase), Bohemia and Silesia being the chief sources of stones. Berlin and Dresden became important centres of production in Germany.

Berlin boxes were often ornamented with relief mosaics in coral, lapis lazuli, mother-of-pearl and ivory. Plain enamelled boxes glistened with diamonds. Frederick took a great interest in the industry, and his own collection contained well over 1,500 snuff boxes. Switzerland also produced very distinctive gold boxes, often featuring enamelled paintings and some, made in Geneva, included timepieces.

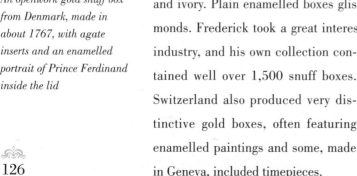

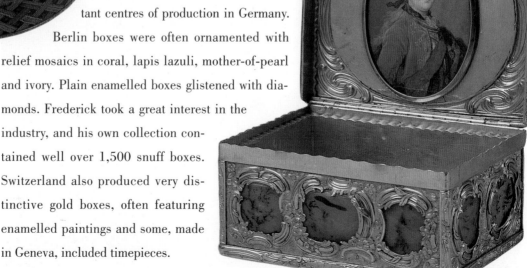

F BOXES

Paul Revere Silverware

RIGHT:

Examples of silverware by Paul Revere include this superb sugar bowl and matching cream pot, made in about 1785.

The craft of silversmithing began to develop in America within a hundred years of the arrival of the first settlers and produced some of the New World's finest treasures. One of the oldest recorded pieces of American silver, dated 1651, is a small dram cup by Robert Sanderson of Boston. This and others from the period are typically English in style. Sanderson had been born in London and worked for some years there before moving to New England.

The earliest American silver was made primarily from melted-down English and Dutch pieces, and it is not surprising that European designs of the time influenced the new work. Gadrooning was a popular style of decoration, in which a series of convex flutes and curves, embellished with small repeating motifs, formed an ornamental pattern or moulding. While Boston silversmiths drew mainly on the English tradition, those from New York were inspired principally by the Netherlands. Many of the greatest names in early New York silverwork are clearly Dutch in origin.

By 1720, the work of American silversmiths consisted of far more than merely copying what was made in Europe. It was gradually developing its own distinctive style, emphasising contour

plain surfaces and rhythmic curves. Most objects were circular, with little decoration besides engraving. American tankards, in particular, were quite distinct from those produced in Europe.

American schoolchildren are taught that Paul Revere was a great patriot who warned of British advances during the Revolutionary War. A famous 19th-century poem by Henry Wadsworth Longfellow celebrated Revere's famous 1773 horse ride to neighbouring towns ('To arms! The British are coming!'). However, Revere would have deserved an honoured place in American history even if he had never proved his worth as a patriot: his work as an engraver and silversmith would always have kept his name alive. His surviving cream jugs, trays, coffeepots and bowls are celebrated in museums today.

Revere was born the son of Apollos Rivoirean, an immigrant Huguenot who landed in Boston in 1715 at the age of 13. Rivoirean, who had been expelled from France along with many other Protestants, took the new name of Paul Revere and served an apprenticeship to one of the 32 goldsmiths in Boston at the time. He passed on the name Paul to his son, who went on to follow in his father's trade.

In 1761 Paul Revere II began the first of his two summary day books, describing his work for wealthy and distinguished patrons, which provide us with not only a detailed record of his career but also a unique insight into the world he inhabited and the craft of a silversmith of the time. He made magnificent solid silver punch bowls, chafing dishes, teapots and salvers in the prevailing London styles, with repoussé, gadrooning, lacy edges and crouching, ornamented legs with feet like paws. He also made a wide variety of smaller objects of exceptional quality and elegance, such as shoe buckles, spoons, earrings, bracelets, sword hilts, babies' rattles and even dog collars.

PEWTER

Pewter is an alloy of tin mixed with copper, with antimony and/or bismuth sometimes added for hardening. (Pure tin is suitable for few purposes, because of both its brittleness and its cost.) Tin mixed with lead has also been used to make pewter, but this produces a material of inferior quality.

Pewter was used in Europe from Roman times until it was largely replaced by electroplating in the 18th and 19th centuries. Early medieval pewter ware included pilgrims' badges and certain items for churches, but from the 14th century onwards pewter was favoured for all kinds of drinking vessels as well as for plates, dishes, bowls, candlesticks and spoons. In North America it has been used since the mid-17th century. The shapes and decorative styles employed in the design of pewter often followed those fashionable in silverware at the time. From the 16th to 18th centuries pewter was frequently elaborate in style, with much repoussé and engraving.

Chinese Table Screens

BELOW:

An 18th-century Chinese jade table screen ornamented with butterflies and chrysanthemums and mounted on an intricate openwork base.

Jade is the name given to the semiprecious stones jadeite and nephrite which can vary in colour from nearly white to very dark green and from reddish-grey to black. Ancient jade shows a wider range of colours than that quarried in recent centuries.

Objects produced during the Chinese Ming dynasty (1368–1644) were marvels of craftsmanship, adorned with dragons, peacocks, lotus flowers, cranes and other animals. Chinese jade carved after the accession of K'ang-hsi in 1662 was modelled mainly with floral patterns. (One way of dating jade from the mid-16th century to the end of the 18th century is by the subtle marks left by the treadle-operated cutting machinery of the time.)

Human figures and animals carved in the round were popular subjects from late in the Ming era until the early 19th century. The phoenix, an omen of harmony and prosperity, was often portrayed perched on a tree, while other animal images included deer, elephants, goats, boars, cats, lions and dogs. Dragons and tigers represented the God of Wealth, and the dragons depicted included some with tiger's claws and others with fish-like scales. They displayed the rich imaginative powers of the artist as well as reflecting the social standing of the owner of the piece. Court etiquette decreed that five-clawed dragons could only be owned by the emperor and his oldest sons.

Goldfish, which the Chinese saw as symbols

of endurance, were popular in the houses of the wealthy, and in the late 18th century the Emperor Ch'ien-lung had a huge goldfish bowl cut from a single lump of jade. Such bowls were usually carved with images of carp or goldfish; twin fish in a carving signified a happy marriage, and bowls of this kind were favoured as wedding presents.

Many other household objects were also made of jade, such as ink jars, pen boxes and paperweights in the form of jade pebbles carved with fighting dragons and other monsters. Tablets of jade, known as table screens, carved with mythical scenes, and set vertically on stands, were made to protect unrolled scrolls from splashes of ink and hold them steady. Similar screens, carved on both sides, sat in windows as ornaments.

The splendour of Chinese jade carvings impressed the Mogul emperors of Hindustan in the 16th and 17th centuries. Workshops were set up in Delhi to extend the tradition, using sage green and white jadeites from Burma as a background for the mounting of emeralds, rubies, lapis lazuli and amethysts against gold foil. Expert Indian carvers and jewel-setters went to Peking in 1741 to teach their techniques, and Chinese craftsmen began producing items like the table screens illustrated.

LEFT:
*Detail from this
magnificent green jade
table screen shows story-
like images of a figure
travelling in a
mountainous, forested
landscape.*

RIGHT:
*This elegant table screen
is inlaid with mother-of-
pearl and tortoiseshell.*

Gena Senin and his Toad

OPPOSITE:
Gena Senin and his toad are depicted here in a carved netsuke. According to legend, Gena's astral body had strayed into the toad.

RIGHT:
A netsuke portraying the Treasure Ship of the Seven Gods of Good Luck, which carried among its cargo the Hammer of Chaos and the Hat of Invisibility.

ash toggles called 'netsuke' provided a way for Japanese men wearing kimonos to carry objects such as inros (see pages 118–19), drinking gourds or tobacco pouches. The relevant item was hung on one end of a cord and the netsuke toggle was fastened to the other end and pushed down securely through the kimono sash. More than one might be worn at a time. Priests and scholars used netsuke to carry their writing equipment; the type of netsuke used would depend on the rank and needs of the wearer.

Tobacco had been introduced into Japan by the Portuguese in the 16th century but it was banned in the 17th century and cultivating tobacco became a punishable offence. As a result, gentlemen and samurai warriors neither smoked nor carried smoking equipment in public at that time. Amongst traders, farmers and labourers, however, smoking became fashionable in spite of the ban, and this gave rise to a demand for tobacco pouches and consequently for netsuke in which to carry them.

The earliest netsuke were merely shells, gourds or tree roots (the word comes from 'ne', a root, and 'tsuke', to fasten). In the 16th century bamboo rings were also adopted as a means of hanging objects from a kimono sash, but by the 18th century practical needs had generated a distinctive art form. Folklore and legends provided a wide variety of popular subjects for magnificent miniatures of people, animals and landscapes, known as 'katabori'. Gena Senin was one such character who was frequently represented in ivory with his toad. While ivory and wood were the most commonly used materials, netsuke were also made from tortoiseshell, coral, enamelled metal, and sometimes horn, shell, jade, amber or even porcelain.

Animals were often portrayed with great humour. In one notable netsuke an octopus is shown flirting with a mermaid. Another shows a drunken creature sleeping off the after-effects of sake. Gamblers wore netsuke in the shape of skulls or snakes to bring them luck. Just as the samurai wore increasingly decorative swords, so wealthy merchants commissioned more elaborate netsuke, and in the 18th and 19th centuries netsuke provided rich expression for the imagination of Japanese carvers. Before 1780 they were made primarily from waste products of other crafts, but they had become a major industry by the late 18th century. Many were signed by their makers and over 2,000 carvers have been listed. In the late 19th century, as cigarettes and western dress became widely adopted, the netsuke declined from general use.

Since Japan has no notable wealth in gemstones, except for some agate, topaz and quartz, it is not surprising that the Japanese have relied more on intricate craftsmanship than on the intrinsic value of the materials used.

The most common form of netsuke was the katabori, which took the form of a small, three-dimensional carving usually showing human or animal figures. However, there were other forms of netsuke such as the kagamibuta, a netsuke with a bowl-shaped ivory, bone or horn receptacle covered by a convex metal disc. These were often valued most highly for their lids, which sometimes incorporated gold, silver and cloisonné. The cord from which these netsuke were hung was held by a loop underneath the metal lid. The production of kagamibuta reached its peak in the late 19th century when the demand for some traditional craftwork, such as the making of samurai swords and sword fittings, was declining.

Another form of netsuke was the manju (it took its name from the round, flat manju bun), which was made in a flattish oval or square shape with rounded corners. The subjects engraved on it included human scenes and animals.

Ashanti Head

Fine artefacts and jewellery were made in the kingdom of Ashanti (now part of Ghana) in the African Gold Coast. There was an abundant supply of gold in this region in the 18th and 19th centuries, and much of it was made into decorative items and apparel for kings and high dignitaries. Kings wore solid gold caps as a symbol of their power, which amazed the Portuguese sea captains who landed on the Ashanti coast. Gold dust could be made into jewellery or objects only with the king's consent, and by controlled artisans who were members of a goldworkers' guild.

Ashanti jewellery – which included discs worn as official insignia, pectorals, bracelets, finger and toe rings and talismans – was often elaborately decorated with repoussé work and chasing. Some items were made by applying gold foil over a wooden core. Similar jewellery was made in neighbouring regions; all of it was known as 'Akan' ware after the name of the common language. The mid-19th century head illustrated here, which is now in the Wallace Collection, London, is an example of the use of 'cire perdue' gold casting (see panel), which was used as early as the 13th century.

Gold dust was the currency of the Ashanti in pre-colonial days, and brass weights for measuring it were produced by the goldsmiths. These too were made by the cire perdue casting method and offer fascinating insights into life at that time. The weights average about 2–3 in (5–8cm) in size and are often decorated with images of people, animals or household objects. Some illustrate an everyday scene or proverb.

Unlike other African kingdoms, Ashanti did not use figures of deceased royalty for ancestor worship. It was thought that a man's spirit lived on in his wooden stool, and the stools of dead chiefs were sometimes plated with gold (or silver if they belonged to a queen mother). These were kept in sacred houses and sacrifices were made before them. According to legend, the Golden Stool of the Ashanti people came from heaven during the 17th century. It was believed to hold the soul of the Ashanti people, and the nation would sicken or die if the stool was lost or destroyed.

In 1817 an agent of the British West Africa Company, T E Bowdich, described the Ashanti city of Kumasi and the 'many gold ornaments which glistened in every direction'. Besides necklaces, anklets and bracelets, he enthused about 'gold and silver pieces which dazzled the eye' and described wolves' and rams' heads cast in gold and suspended from gold-handled swords.

BELOW:

A funerary mask made of wood, brass and copper from Gabon in central west Africa. Such masks were kept by members of the Bakota tribe, together with the bones of their ancestors, to ward off the influence of evil spirits.

RIGHT:

Sometimes described as a mask, this gold Ashanti head from the rich treasure of King Kofi Kakari was brought to England after the First Ashanti War (1873–4).

INSET OPPOSITE:

An Ashanti leather helmet with gold and silver decoration, worn by senior members of the court.

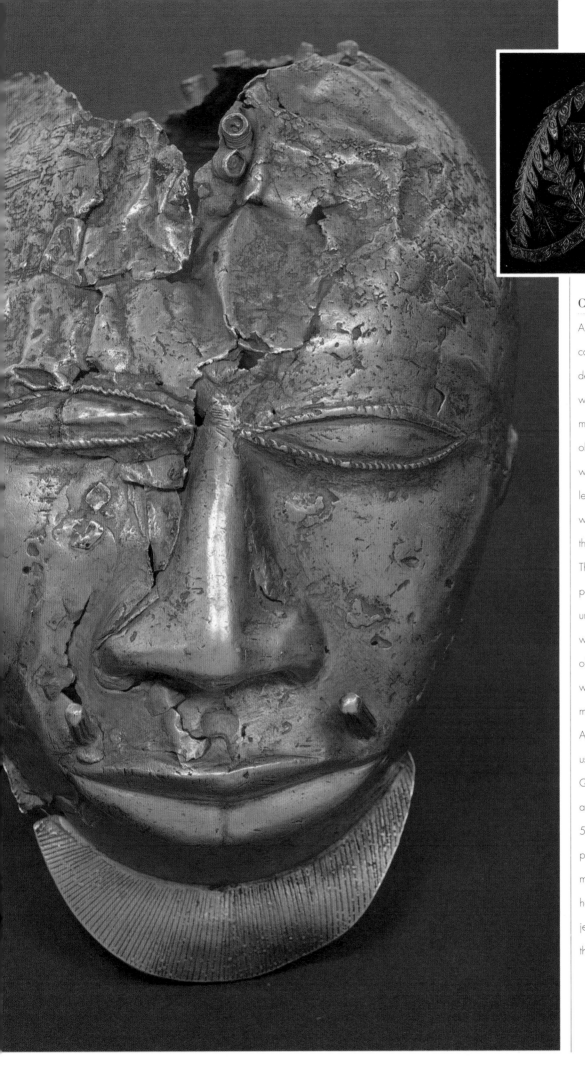

CIRE PERDUE

A sophisticated technique for casting which was first developed in the ancient world, 'cire perdue' literally means 'lost wax'. After an object has been modelled in wax it is coated in clay, leaving a vent through which, when the clay has hardened, the wax can be melted out. The same vent can be used to pour in molten metal. It is uncertain when cire perdue was invented, but some objects in Tutankhamun's tomb were made in this way so it may have been devised by the Ancient Egyptians. It was also used extensively in the Quimbaya area of Colombia and in Peruvian jewellery from 500 to 1500. While cire perdue was originally intended mainly for casting bronze, it has also been used for gold jewellery and objects such as the Ashanti head.

135

Chinese Folding Fan

For many women in past centuries the fan was a weapon in the romantic war. With a flutter or a discreet, slow wave, it could express or conceal her every emotion. Besides being a cooling device and a fashion accessory, the decorated fan was often a work of art.

The word 'fan' is from the Latin *vannus*, meaning a winnowing machine. A distinction must be made between the rigid and folding varieties: the rigid 'screen' fan has a fixed shape attached to a handle, while the more versatile folding fan has a 'leaf' or 'mount' attached to a skeleton of sticks. These sticks are made from a variety of materials, ranging from bone, horn, tortoise-shell and wood to iron, steel and even mother-of-pearl. The two outermost sticks are called 'guards' and their shape is an important clue in accurately dating the fan.

The 'brisé' is a third type of fan which opens but has no leaf. The uncovered sticks overlap slightly and are held together by a ribbon delicately threaded through each one. While usually made from sandalwood, they can also be found in ivory, horn or bone.

The very earliest fans were probably rigid, dating from the 11th century BC in China, Japan and India. The folding fan seems to have evolved in Japan in about the 7th century and spread to China a few centuries later. The fan was then brought to Europe by Portuguese traders in the

15th century and gradually developed a less oriental style. Within Europe, Italy was the leader in fan design until about 1650 when France assumed the prime position.

Fans gradually became larger, and by the mid-18th century the typical stick length was 12in (30cm). This was the heyday of the decorated fan, with 'marriage' fans showing pictures of enthralled

dance fan served as a discreet *aide-mémoire* since it bore printed directions for the dance.

From 1770 onwards fans appeared with more and more elaborate decoration, including sequins, but in the early 19th century they became smaller again and relatively simple. Leaves were generally made of chicken skin, silk or paper mounted on a framework of horn, ivory, bone or wood. In Germany iron sticks were common. 'Mandarin' fans, imported from China, bore miniature scenes from Chinese life.

MOTHER-OF-PEARL

Mother-of-pearl comes from the hard, smooth iridescent lining of the shell of certain molluscs, such as the oyster, abalone, nautilus and river mussel. The iridescence is produced by light reflected off the layers of nacre (the technical name for mother-of-pearl). The colour and lustre of the material varies according to geographical distribution. The rosy type comes from the Pacific and Indian Oceans, while the sea-green variety is found in the Southern Pacific. Mother-of-pearl has been used since ancient times for decoration. Its use in furniture inlay and marquetry achieved special prominence in the 17th century, but two centuries later it became fashionable for fans, card cases, snuff boxes, buttons and inlaid silhouettes.

lovers, while 'mourning' fans depicted urns and weeping willows. One variation was the 'quizzing' fan which had a peephole cleverly worked into the main design. While the user could look through the hole, her face could not be seen. A quadrille

By the early 20th century fans were no longer in constant daytime use, but as an attractive evening accessory their popularity persisted for some time. Swansdown, peacock, osprey and ostrich feather fans remained in vogue until the late 1920s.

Paul Storr Tableware

BELOW:
This silver soup tureen by Paul Storr is one of a pair made in London in 1819–20. It is now in the Victoria and Albert Museum.

One of the greatest English silversmiths of the early 19th century Regency period was Paul Storr, who is principally celebrated for work commissioned to mark British naval and military victories as well as for his many superbly elegant domestic pieces. Impressive collections of his finest silver are now on display at Windsor Castle and also at Buckingham Palace.

Born in 1771, he was apprenticed at the age of 14 to a London silversmith who made mainly neo-classical urns. Storr carried this neo-classical influence into his own later work. Silver tea urns,

some with an ivory tap handle, became an important part of his repertoire. Such urns were heated by inserting a hot iron rod into a central opening.

Tea and coffee sets were a major part of the work produced by silversmiths in the first half of the 19th century. The work of Edward Farrell, another London silversmith, was in marked contrast to the classical sophistication of Storr, usually including human figures and vegetation which he embellished with a great flourish of mixed styles. He is now best remembered for bulbous tea and coffee sets with wavy rims, scrolled handles and elaborate ornamentation.

It was in the middle decades of the 17th century that chocolate, coffee and tea had first been brought to Europe from overseas. The new beverages rapidly created a new drinking fashion and with it a demand for suitable vessels in which to serve them. In England and America silver kettles and kettle stands, tea caddies, coffee and chocolate pots, sugar boxes and creamers, salvers and trays were produced ever more widely in response to this new-found need. Especially popular, both in England and America, were pear-shaped teapots, a practical design which allowed the maximum amount of hot water to mix with the rare and expensive tea leaves at the bottom of the pot.

The introduction of machinery made the pro-

duction of silver cheaper from the mid-18th century onwards. The invention of substitutes also allowed more people to possess what was previously considered a luxury. The first substitute for silver was called Sheffield plate. In 1742 it was discovered that a sheet of copper could be fused by heat to a thin skin of silver. When put through a rolling mill the two metals expanded in unison and could be used like sheet silver at about a fifth of the price. Fused plate was also made in France and Russia.

In 1814 Paul Storr, anticipating another important development in silver processing, made an electrogilt silver goblet, and in 1840 the Elkington cousins of Birmingham were the first to take out patents on the plating industry. In electroplating the object is first made in a base metal, such as copper, and is then put in the plating vat where an electric current is passed through it, covering it in a thin skin of precious metal. By 1836 the copper base had been replaced by a whitish alloy of copper, zinc and nickel and by a metal known as 'Britannia', a mixture of copper, antimony and tin.

Remembrance Jewels

Remembrance jewellery has been worn since ancient times, but it gained special favour in Britain after Prince Albert's death in 1861. The sad mood of the time became widespread and many European women had at least one mourning piece. Mourning jewels were often hung from a band of black velvet which was worn around the neck and crossed at the throat. Because its colour was associated with death, jet became very fashionable. Combined with cut steel, jet was carved into a variety of jewels and ornaments, and, as a substitute, black glass was used in France and Spain in a similar style.

The style of much mid- and late-19th century. They usually contained some treasured item such as a lock of hair or a portrait of a loved one. By the 1870s they had become larger and heavier, and were usually made of gold, silver or pinchbeck with a small photograph of a loved one inside, protected by glass. 'Regard' brooches were given as love tokens, each letter of the word REGARD spelt out in the stone whose name began with the appropriate letter (Ruby, Emerald, Garnet, Amethyst, Ruby and Diamond). By the end of the 19th century lockets of gold, silver and platinum were frequently encrusted with diamonds or pearls, moonstones, turquoises or opals.

The design motifs on early 19th-century jewellery were principally birds, serpents or sometimes stylised flowers made up of precious or semiprecious stones. Gold was treated with great skill, being hand-wrought or, from 1835, stamped out by machines. As many as six shades of gold were produced by adding

ABOVE:
This Renaissance pendant jewel is adorned with precious stones and a hanging pearl.

19th century jewellery was greatly influenced by major discoveries of gold and diamonds, and also by the historical inspiration that came from archeological finds of classical jewellery.

Lockets have been known for centuries, but were at their finest in the

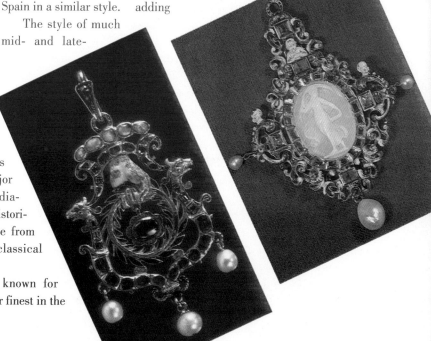

alloys, and the surface was frequently beaded, engraved, etched or studded with gems. It could also be embellished by the skilful use of gold 'cannetille', a type of filigree decoration using very small gold drops.

Popular items of jewellery in Victorian times included long chain necklaces, some reaching almost to the waist and intricately decorated with enamelled serpents or rosettes. Elaborate gold chain ropes were fastened by means of a gold hand (even with a small ring on the forefinger) emerging from an exquisitely detailed lacy cuff.

Rolled gold was invented in 1817, on the same principle as Sheffield plate. Using great heat and pressure, a block of gold is fused on to base metals and rolled repeatedly until the desired thinness is achieved. Rolled gold costs a fraction of real gold and is as light as pinchbeck.

OPPOSITE:
Below, the Aberdeen Jewel holds a lock of hair said to be that of Mary, Queen of Scots, and, centre, a Renaissance pendant with cameo and pearls.

LEFT:
The Gresley Jewel shows portraits of Sir Thomas Gresley and his bride, Catherine Walsingham.

PARURES

Matching sets of jewels, called 'parures', often including a short pendant necklace, a long necklace and a headdress, were fashionable in Europe from the late 16th century to the early 19th century. While the three-piece set was favoured, a parure could consist of almost any number of items. Matching earrings and bracelets were often added in the 19th century. The central feature of a necklace might be detachable to be worn as a brooch, or an elaborate necklace might be constructed in such a way that it could be dismantled and turned into a parure made up of a shorter necklace, one or two brooches and a bracelet. Queen Elizabeth I was a great devotee of parures.

141

Indian Turban Jewel

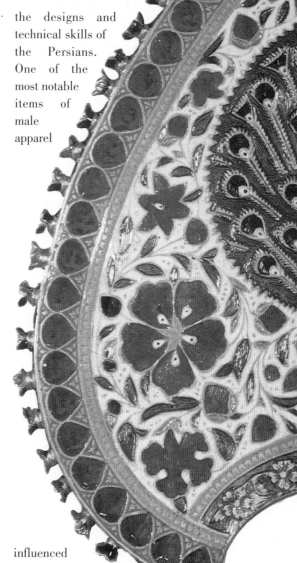

Colourful gemstones have played a central part in the jewellery of south-east Asia for thousands of years. Ancient civilisations of India, Burma, Sri Lanka and Thailand made use of gold, but precious stones were more plentiful than precious metals in these areas; colour was consequently given greater prominence than metal, which was seen as merely providing a frame in which to display gemstones to their best advantage.

In the 3rd millennium BC, when the Sumerians occupied Mesopotamia, the rich culture of Harappa evolved in the Indus Valley. The people of the region did not bury their dead with worldly goods, so little remains of their metals and jewels, but images and carvings reveal their love of personal adornment. Frescoes of the 5th century AD in the Ajanta caves pictured Harappa women garlanded with jewels ranging from headdresses, hoop earrings and necklaces with rows of pendants to arm bands and even leg ornaments. Indian jewellery dating from 330–27 BC, found at Taxila, is ornamented with floral patterns, elephants and peacocks, with many different stones being used on each object.

The rulers of the Mogul Empire, which was established in the 16th century, employed many of the designs and technical skills of the Persians. One of the most notable items of male apparel influenced by Persian style was the turban, which was often encrusted with jewels and fastened with a gem-set Kalgi (aigrette). Paintings reveal that Mogul princes also wore necklaces of precious stones and pearls, earrings, bracelets, sashes with jewels, and

ABOVE:
This delicately enamelled cloisonné gold locket from Jaipur was made in about 1700 to hold perfume.

numerous finger rings. The most impressive aspect of Mogul jewellery was the size and quality of the gemstones used. Legendary tales described emeralds the size of eggs and rubies as big as walnuts, and these

stories were very possibly based on fact. The splendid turban ornament illustrated follows the tradition of brightly coloured Mogul jewellery.

Indian women of the time wore an even wider range of precious ornaments, each with a traditionally designated place on the head or body. Rows of pearls were entwined in the hair and gold bands worn across the forehead, while earrings consisted of strings of pearls hung on gold wire, and discs of gold with stones in the centre. Armbands, worn three or four at a time, took the form of square gold straps embellished with jewels,

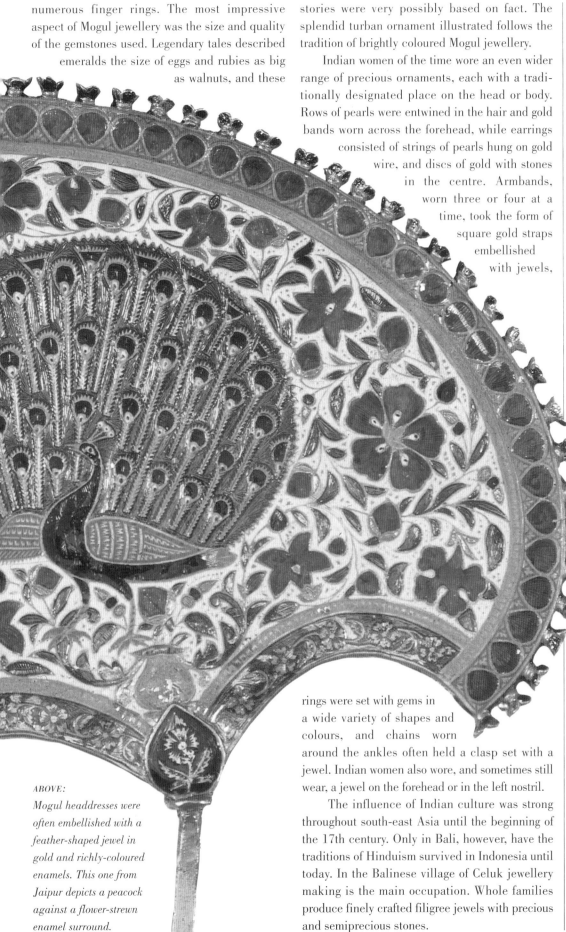

ABOVE:
Mogul headdresses were often embellished with a feather-shaped jewel in gold and richly-coloured enamels. This one from Jaipur depicts a peacock against a flower-strewn enamel surround.

rings were set with gems in a wide variety of shapes and colours, and chains worn around the ankles often held a clasp set with a jewel. Indian women also wore, and sometimes still wear, a jewel on the forehead or in the left nostril.

The influence of Indian culture was strong throughout south-east Asia until the beginning of the 17th century. Only in Bali, however, have the traditions of Hinduism survived in Indonesia until today. In the Balinese village of Celuk jewellery making is the main occupation. Whole families produce finely crafted filigree jewels with precious and semiprecious stones.

RUBIES

Rubies are a variety of a transparent corundum whose colour ranges from pink to deep red. The main source of deep red rubies is the Mogok Valley in Upper Burma, which produces the finest stones in the world (the traditional title of the king of Burma was 'Lord of the Rubies'). Sri Lanka is noted for the pink and light red varieties and Thailand for dark, brownish-red stones. Rubies are one of the most precious of gems, exceeded in value only by emeralds. They have been associated with south east Asia for hundreds of years. Even in the 13th century Sri Lanka (then called 'Zeilan') was noted for them: according to Marco Polo, King Sander-naz of Zeilan owned a legendary ruby 9in (25cm) long, as thick as a man's arm and flawless. Huge formations of ruby have been found, so the stone described by the great Venetian traveller could indeed have existed.

143

Navaho Silver

BELOW:
This silver and torquoise box is a fine example of Navaho craftsmanship, now in the National Museum of the American Indian.

The tribe of native Americans known to outsiders as the Navaho (their name for themselves is Diné, meaning 'the Folks' or 'the People') travelled to what is now the southern United States from Alaska and north-western Canada betwee 900 and 1200. The Navaho traditionally depended on sheep rearing, introduced by the Spanish, and are famous for woven blankets, rugs and other woollen items. Their main art form is silver and turquoise jewellery, again of Spanish influence. They melted down American silver dollars in order to acquire raw material until defacing United States currency was prohibited, when they turned to Mexican pesos as an alternative source of silver.

The Navaho make both hammered and sand-cast jewellery. Hammered silver is made by pounding the metal into a thin layer for cutting, stamping or filing. In sandcasting, a soft rock from which the interior has been carved out in the shape of the design is used to make a mould. Melted silver is then poured into the mould and allowed to harden. Once removed, the silver is then filed and polished.

Using only simple tools and basic methods, the Navaho have produced some magnificent items. The 'squash-blossom' necklace, a classic of Navaho design, was adapted from a Mexican costume decoration in the early 1800s. A 'naja is a

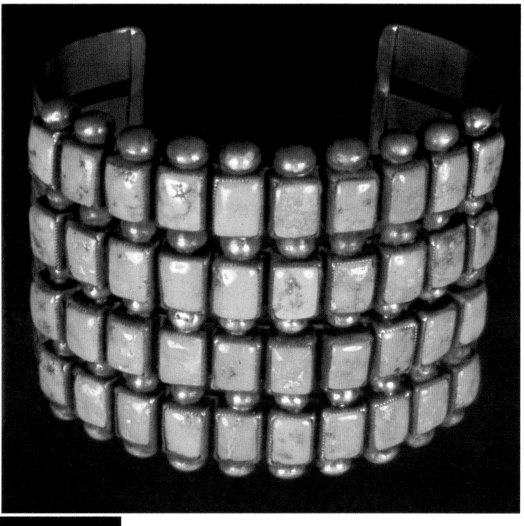

TURQUOISE

Formerly called 'Turkish stone', turquoise takes its name from the Old French 'pierre turqueise'. It has been used as a gemstone for many centuries. The most famous mines were in Khorasan in Iran, with others in Turkestan and the Sinai peninsula. The oldest mines in the United States are near Santa Fé. Jewellery set with turquoises has been found in Egyptian and Sumerian tombs, and as far afield as Mexico and Tibet. The Romans regarded the stone as fit to be carved with an emperor's head. Because turquoise is usually opaque, it is often cut en cabochon. It is especially striking used in combination with silver, as this Navaho jewellery illustrates, as do many modern pieces from Mexico, Tibet and Iran.

crescent-shaped pendant worn suspended from a squash-blossom necklace. The terminals of these pendants are often decorated with rounded buttons, discs or other motifs. A piece of turquoise or some other form of silver ornament is usually suspended within the arc of the naja. A similar contemporary necklace is a 'pomegranate' necklace.

By the 19th century, the Navaho had lived a settled lifestyle in Arizona for hundreds of years, but within a generation they had lost nearly everything. In 1864 they were forced to move to the region of Fort Sumner, in the plains of eastern New Mexico. However, in 1868 a treaty allowed them to resettle in a reservation, and the government gave them 35,000 sheep and goats to encourage a pastoral lifestyle.

The Navaho now have the largest Indian reservation in the United States, covering an area larger than Belgium. It occupies most of north-eastern Arizona and spills over into north-western New Mexico and south-eastern Utah, a diverse landscape of arid desert and pine-clad mountains. While the Navaho have become assimilated into modern America (driving pick-up trucks and wearing baseball caps), they have their own legal system and police, and Navaho is still the native tongue. Unemployment is very high and life expectancy low by American standards. Most of the 100,000 Navaho live today on smallholdings as shepherds and farmers. Craftspeople earn a meagre livelihood by selling goods from stands along the highways or in tourist shops, but thousands of Navahos work away from home, either on lands along the lower Colorado River or in urban areas such as Los Angeles and Kansas City.

ABOVE:
A Navaho bracelet or armlet comprising four bands of silver set with rectangular torquoises between polished silver 'pearls'. It is displayed in the National Museum of the American Indian.

Tiffany Magnolia Vase

The splendid Magnolia Vase, fashioned in silver, gold, enamels and opals, was made by Tiffany and Co in 1893. Now America's leading jewellers, the firm was founded in New York in 1837 under the name of Tiffany, Young and Ellis. It started by selling a variety of items, from stationery and umbrellas to lacquerware, most of which were imported, and its stock included more curiosities and gadgets than fine jewels.

Gradually, however, one of the founders of the firm, C L Tiffany, decided to specialise in quality items, and began selling jewellery made by the goldsmiths of Paris, London and Rome, as well as watches, clocks, bronzes and silverware. When a new tariff of 30 per cent was levied on imported goods in 1844, the company began producing its own silver goods. Tiffany insisted on the same sterling quality (925 parts to 1,000) as was used in England, which was much higher than most American silver at the time.

By the mid-19th century the firm had made shrewd business moves and was prospering. When the older Young and Ellis retired in 1853 it was left

with its single leader and the name Tiffany and Co. Wealthy Americans, from the Astors to the Vanderbilts, became regular patrons, buying silver, jewels, diamonds and long ropes of oriental pearls, and during the Civil War the opportunistic Tiffany supplied soldiers with badges, gold braid and swords. In 1870 a new Tiffany store opened in New York with a stock of jewels valued at over two million dollars, silver valued at a million-and-a-half, and an entire floor devoted to bronzes, clocks and various jewelled curiosities.

In 1877 a mineralogist, George Frederick Kunz, joined the firm. His enthusiasm for semi-precious stones was contagious, with the result that many lesser-known stones such as tourmalines, topazes and garnets soon became almost as popular as diamonds. In 1887 Tiffany's acquired some of the French Crown Jewels; the company's precious vaults now contained precious stones worth over 40 million dollars.

Many of the superb items of silver and jewellery on sale in the store were still imported but many others were being made in New York by the firm's own craftsmen. Among those produced for women were a wide variety of brooches, earrings, bangles, bracelets and lockets: charm bracelets set with coloured stones and studded with diamonds; pendant brooches made with diamonds and carbuncles (garnets set en cabochon); turquoise brooches set in diamond surrounds and often pavé-set to form a spray of flowers. Settings were mainly of gold, and much jewellery was made of enamelled gold, coloured either dark blue, emerald green or ruby red. For men there were watches, chains, rings and seals. After 1892, Tiffany's son, Louis Comfort Tiffany, became famous in his own right for jewellery made of stained or iridescent Favrile glass and for other imaginative glass objects.

BELOW:

Contemporary with Tiffany's Magnolia Vase is this elegant silver and enamel box designed by Archibald Knox for Liberty & Co.

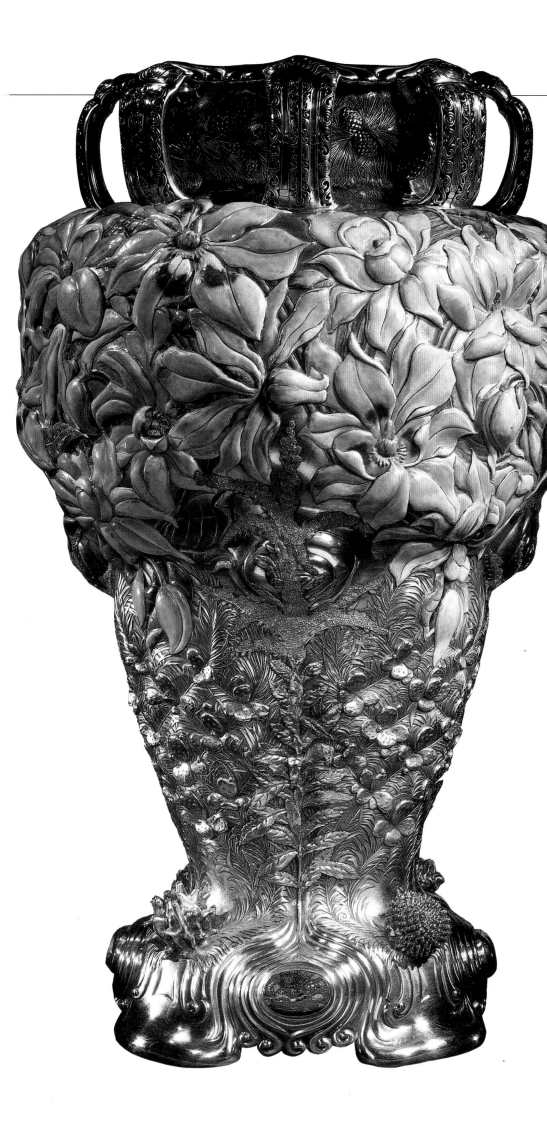

OPALS

Opals – the name itself comes from the Sanskrit word 'upala' meaning gem – are made up of deposits found in many types of sedimentary rock. Their characteristic opalescence and play of delicate hues is caused by the diffraction of light by close-packed silica spheres within the stone. Precious or 'noble' opals are iridescent while common opals are generally lustrous and milky white (though they may be yellow, red, blue, green or black). Opals are usually cut en cabochon but are sometimes faceted or engraved. They first achieved popularity in the 19th century. Hungary was the main source of supply until opals were found in Austria in 1949 and later in Mexico, which is noted for red fire opals. Most now come from Australia, where black opals were discovered in 1905.

LEFT:
The Tiffany Magnolia Vase, shimmering with precious metals, enamels and opals, reflected the opulent style of the late 1800s. It is now displayed in New York's Metropolitan Museum of Art.

F A B E

JEWELLER TO THE TSARS

Peter Carl Fabergé (1846–1920) was a Russian of French descent who became the foremost gold-smith of his time. His father was a successful jeweller in St Petersburg and Peter took command of the family business while still in his mid-twenties. As a craftsman for the imperial Russian court he created sumptuous jewels and ornaments for Tsars Alexander III and Nicholas II. Using gold, silver, lapis lazuli, mala-chite, jade and various precious gems, Fabergé created a remarkable and imaginative range of decorative objects.

He became the darling of royalty and the aristocracy not only in Russia but throughout much of Europe, India and the Orient. By 1898 he was employing over 700 craftsmen in St Petersburg, Moscow, Kiev, Odessa and London, but he always retained control of the work and every piece is distinctly his own in style. Some are very simple, notably his cigarette boxes with their plain ribbed gold lids and thumb-piece opening featur-ing a single gemstone. Others, such as clocks, fans, cups, trays, boxes, icons and jewellery, combined familiar materials in unusual ways to create highly original effects.

With the start of World War I Fabergé's workshops were expropriated by the Communists and turned over to the manufacture of small arms and medical supplies. Fabergé merely asked for ten minutes to 'put on my hat and coat'. He died in Lausanne in 1920, a disillusioned man exiled from both his native country and the dreamlike world he had created.

FABERGÉ'S EGGS

In 1883 Fabergé suggested to Tsar Alexander III that he should give a jewelled Easter egg to the young Tsarina. When the Tsar agreed, Fabergé promised that the egg would contain a surprise. The plain white enamelled egg opened to reveal a gold yolk and a tiny chicken in different coloured golds. Inside this was a model of the imperial crown containing a small egg-shaped ruby. The Tsar was so amazed and delighted that Fabergé was given a standing order for eggs every Easter. He responded with infinite ingenuity and skill, producing a series of minutely detailed and delicate eggs whose surprises ranged from clocks to a model of the Trans-Siberian Express. During World War I his craftsmen had orders to

ABOVE, RIGHT AND BELOW:
Fabergé pocket watches in
coloured enamels and gold

148

adorn the Easter eggs with warlike ornamentation; one egg, produced in gunmetal, was supported on artillery shells.

Coated in translucent yellow enamel and enclosed in a cage-mounted trelliswork of green-gold laurel leaves, the Coronation Egg is ornamented with double-headed eagles in yellow gold enamelled in black, each one set with a rose diamond. It is dated 1897 and was presented to Empress Alexandra by Nicholas II; it bears the empress's monogram in rose diamonds and cabochon rubies. The surprise within the shell is a replica of the imperial coach used in 1896 at the coronation of Nicholas and Alexandra in Moscow. The tiny coach is perfectly articulated and detailed: two steps can be let down when the door opens and pale blue enamelled curtains hang behind the upholstered seats.

ABOVE:
Tsar Nicholas II's monogrammed box, fashioned in gold, enamel and diamonds

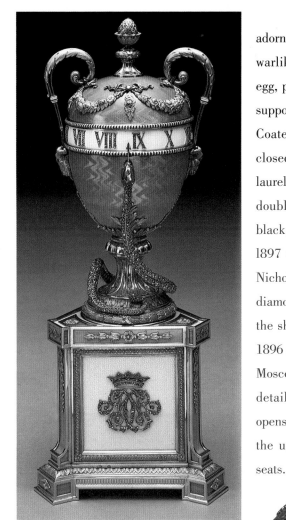

ABOVE:
The Duchess of Marlborough Egg

BELOW AND RIGHT:
The Coronation Egg and coach presented to Empress Alexandra

Art Nouveau Jewellery

In the 1890s and early 1900s the international style known as art nouveau blossomed in the decorative and applied arts of Europe and America. In England it was associated with the designs commissioned by the London store Liberty & Co, for whom designers such as Archibald Knox produced jewellery and fine silverware. In Italy art nouveau is still referred to as the Stile Liberty.

BELOW:
Multi-coloured diamonds adorn this small flower spray brooch.

RIGHT:
A pair of enamel ladybird earclips by Cartier, and a diamond-encrusted butterfly.

OPPOSITE, BELOW:
A hair comb made by jeweller Fred Partridge in horn, enamelled copper and moonstones.

(In German-speaking countries it was called Jugendstil or Sezessionstil.) While the style varied somewhat from place to place, it was characterised by graceful curvilinear and asymmetrical shapes drawn from nature, its most popular images including forms of sea life, snakes, insects and plants. The human figure was usually represented by a willowy, dreamlike woman with long, flowing tresses.

The impetus behind art nouveau, which had its roots in the British Arts and Crafts Movement, was a desire to raise standards of craftsmanship as a reaction to the mass-produced goods manufactured since the Industrial Revolution. While only short-lived, the art nouveau movement paved the way for new developments in art and architecture: artists could never completely break from the past, but they could move away from the historicism and copying of past styles which had dominated 19th-century applied art and produce original work of genius.

Jewellery of the 1890s provides some of the finest examples of the art nouveau style, demonstrating an inspiring approach to design and great concern for quality craftsmanship. It also marked a renaissance of the individual artist-jeweller and a rejection of the traditions of large commercial firms which had begun to dominate jewellery making in the 19th century.

Belgium's most distinguished art nouveau craftsman-designer and jeweller was Philippe Wolfers, whose technical skills compared with

MOONSTONES

One of the cheapest of translucent stones available to jewellers is the milky moonstone. This is a variety of orthoclase, a type of rock-forming mineral known as feldspar. Like other feldspars, the moonstone is always cut en cabochon. The common moonstone is whiter than high-quality stones, which tend to be tinged with blue. The stone's blue-white sheen has led to an association with the moon and in the past it was thought to absorb the moon's rays and banish nightmares. Its pearly, evanescent quality made it a firm favourite with the artisans of art nouveau. The term 'black moonstone' is in fact a misnomer for a dark type of labradorite, while 'pink moonstone' is really a pink scapolite. Remarkable properties have been associated with the moonstone, such as enabling the wearer to predict the future. It is linked to thirteenth anniversaries, and is believed by some people to neutralise any bad luck associated with that number.

those of René Lalique (see page 152). Wolfers was born into a family of jewellers and learned the trade from his father. Like others in the 1890s, he turned to nature for inspiration, but one of his most striking talents was his unusual juxtaposition of materials and his clever use of irregularities in semiprecious stones.

The Frenchman Georges Fouquet also came from a family of jewellers and took over his family firm in 1895. He found an excellent art nouveau partner in the Czechoslovakian graphic artist Alphonse Mucha, who worked in Paris. Two of the most striking results of their collaboration are a remarkable parure de corsage, featuring a carved ivory face surrounded by flowing hair in ivory and gold, and a bracelet and ring made for Sarah Bernhardt.

Eugene Feuillatre, yet another great talent flourishing in the years of art nouveau, worked in the workshop of René Lalique before setting up on his own in 1899. He specialised in techniques for enamelling on silver and platinum and in 'plique a jour' enamelling (see page 153). Besides jewels, he made unusual bottles, dishes and other objects.

TOP:
An enamel and soapstone pendant in the form of a butterfly's wings enclosing a woman's upturned face.

The largest public collection of art nouveau jewels is now in the Museé des Arts Décoratifs in Paris, though most of the items are kept in the museum vaults.

Lalique Jewellery

ABOVE RIGHT:

The extraordinary delicacy and size of the Lalique dragonfly – it has a wingspan of over 10in (25cm) – makes it especially striking. It is made of gold mixed with chrysoprase (an apple-green chalcedony) and the finest enamel work.

RIGHT:

One of the most striking and unusual of Lalique's insect creations is this magnificent wasp cluster in which he used translucent enamel and gold to remarkable effect. It is one of the most spectacular jewels of the late 1800s.

Agreat genius of art nouveau style, the French craftsman René Lalique produced some of the most original and exciting jewellery ever made. His subjects were usually drawn from nature – plants, fish and animals – and the remarkably intricate and well-observed pieces shown here reflect his special fascination with insects. At times he would faithfully reproduce nature with great precision while at others he distorted reality and created fanciful images of great imaginative charm. On close examination, the 'dragonfly' corsage brooch illustrated above turns out to be a strange insect-like creature with a long, tapering body and enormous claws, surmounted by a nude female torso with huge wings made of flexible plique-a-jour (see panel).

Lalique originally wanted to be a painter but in 1876, at the age of 16, he became apprenticed to an eminent Parisian jeweller, Aucoc. After two years Lalique went to England and, having returned to Paris in 1881, opened his own workshop to experiment with innovative techniques and styles.

For Lalique, the value of a piece of jewellery had nothing to do with the intrinsic cost of the materials used. He was passionate about glass and enamel, and combined these in unconventional ways with other materials such as ivory, horn and amber, which he carved with great skill and artistry. He also freely mixed different coloured golds and diamonds with glass, silver, copper, steel and even aluminium.

It was a commission from the actress Sarah Bernhardt in 1891 that gave a major boost to his career – Bernhardt, who became an important patron of Lalique, was very partial to large, dramatic jewellery – and within another five years his work was acclaimed on the Paris fashion scene.

Another major supporter and admirer of Lalique was the Armenian oil millionaire Calouste Gulbenkian, who lived in Paris and London and met Lalique through Sarah Bernhardt. It was his sponsorship that made much of Lalique's best work possible and it was he who commissioned Lalique to put together a collection in 1898. He loaned the famous dragonfly brooch to Sarah Bernhardt to wear on several occasions. The Gulbenkian Foundation in Lisbon – where many of the most exquisite examples of Lalique jewellery, including the dragonfly corsage brooch, can be seen today – has the finest collection of art nouveau jewellery in the world.

In 1909 Lalique bought a glass factory at Combes la Ville and glass became increasingly prominent in his jewellery designs. In 1914 he gave up the making of jewellery completely to devote himself exclusively to the creation of objects in glass.

LEFT:
Nude women were a common theme in Lalique's work, though in some of his pieces he focused simply on a female head with great swirls of hair, a popular art nouveau image.

PLIQUE-A-JOUR

The technique called plique-a-jour uses transparent enamels to create an effect similar to stained-glass. Unlike cloisonné, the cells into which the enamel is poured have no backs so light passes through them. One plique-a-jour method mixed a flux into the enamel to prevent it from running. Another, more common, practice was to attach an openwork metal mount to a sheet of copper foil. The cells were filled with enamel and left to harden, and the copper was then dissolved by putting the piece in acid. Craftsmen had used this technique in the 15th century, but it is now mainly associated with jewellery of the 19th century – and especially with the remarkable genius of René Lalique. What most set Lalique above other art nouveau jewellers was the boldness of his fantasies and the exceptionally wide range of materials that he used.

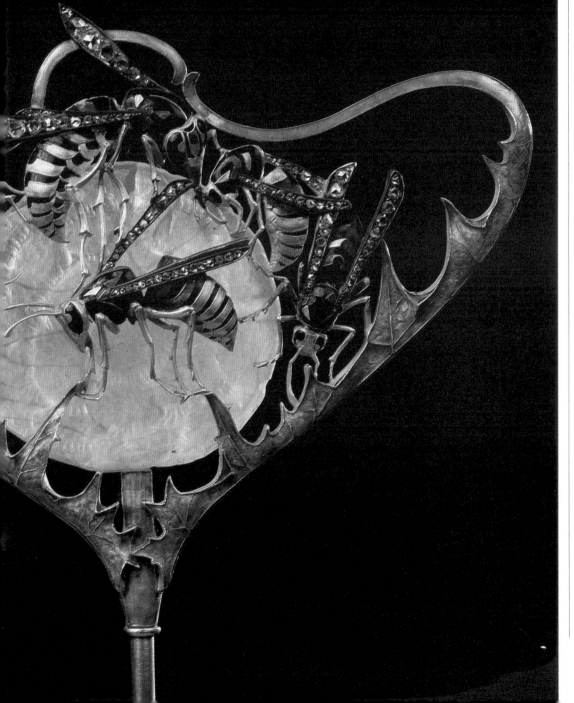

The Cartier Bracelet

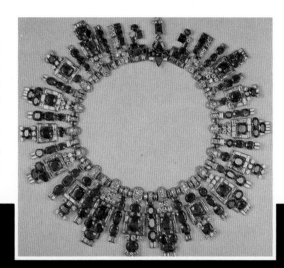

*D*esigns in jewellery are often affected by current trends in other art forms, and, when the influences of the art nouveau movement began to decline at the start of World War I, their place was taken by Bauhaus and cubist trends, which dominated the art world during the 1920s and early 1930s. The fashion in jewellery was increasingly for geometric designs, like the elegant crystal bracelet shown here.

BELOW:
A superb art deco-style bracelet in crystal, platinum and sapphires, made in 1925.

The famous jewellery firm of Cartier was founded in 1847 by Louis-François Cartier. In the early days it made jewels of enamelled gold set with gemstones, which attracted a prestigious clientele – including Edward VII, members of the French and Brazilian royal families and the grand dukes of Russia. In more recent times the firm has widened its scope to embrace other styles of jewellery and has worldwide operations.

The Cartier necklace illustrated has exceptionally fine matching rubies mixed with brilliant- and baguette-cut diamonds. The brilliant-cutting technique, invented by a Venetian lapidary, Vincenzo Peruzzi, at the end of the 17th century, entails cutting the stone with 56 facets to make the most of its reflective properties. Baguette-cutting is used for small diamonds, generally side stones arranged around a larger specimen.

It is the rise of diamonds from the end of the 17th century that has been the single most important factor in the design of modern jewellery. From this point onwards personal ornaments became dominated by faceted gems, and stones mounted en cabochon declined in fashion. Even gold assumed a secondary role, acting more as a link and surround for faceted stones.

Diamonds had been exported from India since early times, but were very rare. Organised mining started in about 600 BC in an area known as Golconda in Hyderabad; the Portuguese were probably the first Europeans to visit these mines,

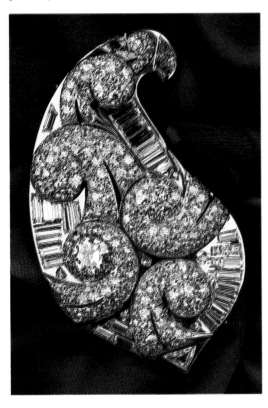

in 1565. The Koh-i-noor (see page 106) is one of the most famous stones to have been mined at Golconda. Towards the end of the 17th century Indian diamond production declined sharply and is now relatively insignificant. Brazilian diamonds, discovered in about 1725, were virtually exhausted by 1894, but in 1869 the first South African diamonds had appeared on the Paris market, and the creation of precious jewellery was unthinkable without them by the late 1800s. South Africa remains one of the principal sources of gem-quality diamonds found today.

Diamonds had been cut efficiently as early as the 14th century but, by the 18th century, table, rose- and even brilliant-cut diamonds were common and cutting had become a major activity in the cities of Antwerp and Amsterdam.

The strength of platinum made open-backed settings popular after 1910, and new ways of setting such as this placed emphasis on the stone itself rather than the setting. In the 1920s the squares and triangles which appeared in pre-war cubist paintings began to be reflected in large rectangular and pyramidal jewels – emerald-cut and baguette-cut stones – whose three-dimensional quality made them especially dramatic. In 1962 the Diamond Polishing Works Ltd of London invented the 'princess cut', now known as the 'profile', and the following year the 'highlight' cut of 74 facets was invented in South Africa.

PLATINUM

The silvery-white metal known as platinum was used in Colombia and Ecuador before the 15th century. It became available in Europe after 1730, but its high melting point (1773°F/967°C) discouraged its use. However, in 1847 an American scientist, Robert Hare, invented an oxy-hydrogen blowpipe which allowed it to be worked much more easily, and by about 1900 platinum had become extremely popular for jewellery. It is very malleable, does not tarnish and is so strong that little is needed for setting stones. It is generally mixed with other metals to make an alloy. Japan is now one of the world's main consumers of platinum for jewellery.

Dali's Eye of Time

ABOVE:

Dali's 'Eye of Time' is made of gold with diamonds and a single ruby.

156

Born in 1904 near Barcelona, Salvador Dali is best known as a 20th-century Spanish surrealist painter but he dabbled in a variety of the visual arts – printmaking, theatrical design and jewellery – as well as film producing. His personal style evolved after meeting Picasso and surrealist painters in the late 1920s. He described his work as 'hand-painted dream photographs' and his purpose as being 'to systematize confusion and thus to help discredit completely the world of reality'.

Dali's first pieces of jewellery were commissioned by Eric Ertman of Finland and a number were shown at the Milan Triennale in 1954. Between the early 1950s and 1969 he made sketches in watercolour for some remarkable and highly original modern designs in metals and gems. Besides pieces for ordinary wear, Dali produced large sculptural creations with parts oper-

Great Treasures of the World

ated by small electric motors. While he revelled in bizarre, dream-like images, he also had great admiration for the old Italian masters, once commenting that his jewellery was a 'protest against the high cost of jewellery materials. My aim is to show the jeweller's art in its true perspective – where the design and the craftsmanship are of more value than the gems, as in the Renaissance era.'

Dali's celebrated painted image of limp, melted watches in *The Persistence of Memory* was also realised as a piece of jewellery. Finding inspiration after eating camembert cheese, he commented that 'the famous soft clocks are merely the soft, crazy, lonely camembert of time and space'. The Owen Cheatham Foundation in New York City owns a major collection of Dali's jewels.

Other famous 20th-century artists, such as Georges Braque and Pablo Picasso, also worked in metals and precious stones. By 1909 Braque and Picasso were pioneers of the cubist style which influenced not only their paintings but also their designs for jewellery. In 1963 the Museé des Arts Décoratifs exhibited 133 jewels designed by Braques and executed by Baron Henri-Michel Heger de Lowenfeld. From the mid-1940s Picasso modelled medallions with bulls' heads in terracotta, some of which were then cast in gold. After visiting a dentist in 1952 Picasso was prompted to design a gold necklace which he said was inspired by the dental processes.

Other modern artists who applied their talents to jewellery design include Max Ernst, Dubuffet,

The brass wire necklace above was designed and made by Alexander Calder c1938 while, below, is 'Les Fils d'Eos', a brooch in gold, lapis lazuli and diamonds made by Georges Braque.

Arp, Man Ray, Giacometti and, arguably one of the most important, the American Alexander Calder, who became famous for his sculptured mobiles. In the late 1930s he began designing a variety of brooches and necklaces using strips of gold and silver wire. Jean Cocteau also created distinctive pieces in which he skilfully combined gold with enamels, rubies and diamonds.

CUBISM AND SURREALISM

In 1911 cubism became the official label of a new art movement of which Braque and Picasso were the key figures. As Braque said later, they were 'like two mountaineers roped together', exploring a new territory in which objects are depicted as they are known and not as they appear. While cubism was not meant to be abstract art, it did represent the world in a less than literal way. The influence of cubism was felt widely in international design, and aspects of its two-dimensional geometry can be seen in art deco jewellery of the 1920s and 1930s. Dali joined the Surrealist movement in 1929, but its foundations had already been laid in 1924 by André Breton, who wrote about the mental point 'at which real and imaginary, past and future cease to be perceived in contradiction', and which surrealism aimed to explore.

157

Georg Jensen Necklace

Founded in 1904, the Danish firm of Georg Jensen silversmiths now has many branches worldwide. Its founder, Georg Jensen (1866–1935), became known for his stylish jewellery in the early 20th century, using silver, amber and semiprecious stones. Jensen's son and later chief designer, Soren Georg, advanced the firm's reputation for sterling silver tableware, ornaments and jewellery; in recent years Jensen's has made gold and silver jewellery in simple styles, often set with gemstones.

Another important modern figure in this field is Gilbert Albert, a leading Swiss designer-maker of watches and jewellery. He was chief designer for the company Patek Philippe from 1954 and later for Omega before opening his own workshop in Geneva in 1962. He held a one-man show at Goldsmiths Hall in London in 1965, the first modern artist to do so. His special interest has been the design of abstract gold jewellery, like the gold pendant watch shown.

Since 1964 Albert has made brooches and other items from fragments of meteorites and objects of little material value – the modern trend is to create treasures in which the intrinsic value of the materials used is secondary to the aesthetic worth of the piece.

Over the last 5,000 years the workmanship involved in making precious objects with metals and gems has changed surprisingly little. Most of

ABOVE:
Gilbert Albert's watch is concealed beneath a lid covered with baroque pearls.

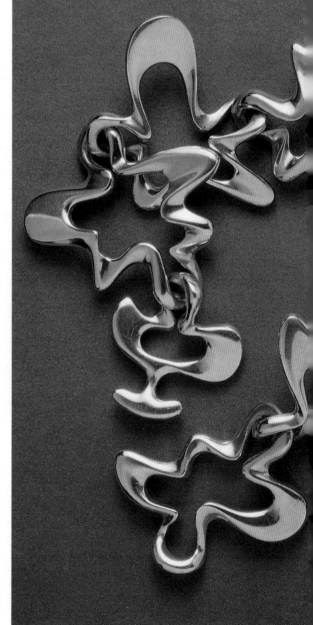

the techniques used today have been practised by ancient civilisations, and the forms created (from necklaces, rings and earrings to bowls, decorated weapons and religious objects) have remained much the same.

What has changed is that, since the 18th century, precious ornaments, jewels and other such treasures have become available to more people as mass production has become possible. With increasing prosperity the great jewel houses have expanded into larger markets, bringing jewellery within reach of more people than ever before. Another change is that greater recognition has been given to female jewellers, such as Madame

Belperoon of Paris who produced elegant and original jewellery between the wars. More recently Wendy Renshaw has become known for silver rings with stones that create a different pattern by altering the order in which they are worn together. Helga Zhan has also acquired a name for the large, bold shapes of her silver jewellery.

Although much has been lost, at least some of the wonderful objects created over the centuries have been preserved by museums, galleries and private collections. Objects with symbolic importance as well as aesthetic appeal, these treasures are a valuable reminder of human ingenuity and talent throughout the ages.

GREAT MODERN JEWELLERS

Among the most prestigious modern jewellery firms are Asprey of London, Black, Starr and Frost of New York, Bulgari of Rome and Boucheron of Paris. Harry Winston of New York was, until his death in 1978, the world's largest individual dealer in diamonds. He handled or owned 60 of the world's 303 listed major diamonds.

The world-famous Paris firm of Van Cleef & Arpels, which also deals in priceless jewels, made the crown for the empress of Iran's coronation in 1967. The centrepiece of the crown was a magnificent 150-carat emerald, surrounded by an impressive array of 1,469 diamonds, 36 rubies, 36 emeralds and 105 pearls. It may seem that the great age of glittering jewellery is over, but spectacular treasures of this kind are still being created.

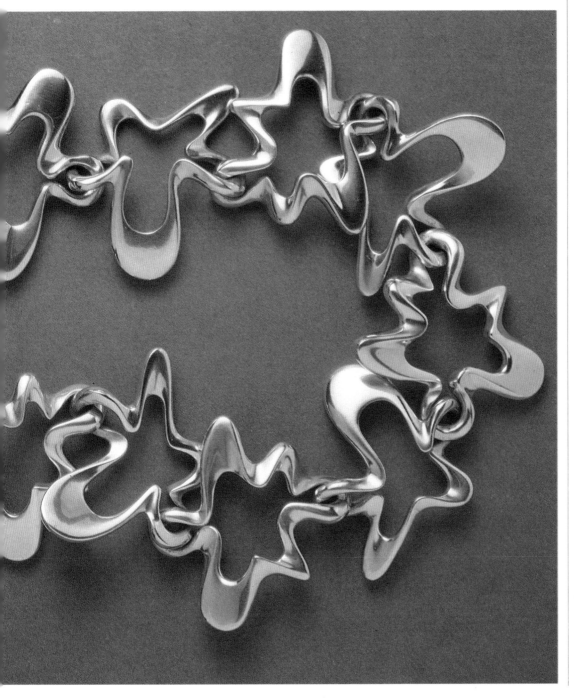

LEFT:
This necklace, made by the firm of Georg Jensen and designed by Henning Koppel, emphasises that artistic treasures can be very simply styled.

Index

Page numbers in italics refer to illustrations